OVETA CULP HOBBY

Oveta Culp Hobby

Colonel, Cabinet Member, Philanthropist

★

BY DEBRA L. WINEGARTEN

UNIVERSITY OF TEXAS PRESS, AUSTIN

The Louann Atkins Temple Women & Culture Series is supported by Allison, Doug, Taylor, and Andy Bacon; Margaret, Lawrence, Will, John, and Annie Temple; Larry Temple; the Temple-Inland Foundation; and the National Endowment for the Humanities.

LIBRARY OF CONGRESS
CATALOGING-IN-PUBLICATION DATA

Winegarten, Debra L.
    Oveta Culp Hobby : colonel, cabinet member, philanthropist / by Debra L. Winegarten.
        pages   cm — (Louann Atkins Temple women & culture series)
    Includes bibliographical references and index.
    ISBN 978-0-292-72268-2

1. Hobby, Oveta Culp, 1905–1995. 2. United States. Department of Health, Education, and Welfare—Biography. 3. Cabinet officers—United States—Biography. 4. United States. Army. Women's Army Corps—Officers—Biography. 5. United States. War Department. Bureau of Public Relations. Women's Interest Section—Biography. 6. World War, 1939–1945—Participation, Female. 7. World War, 1939–1945—Women—United States. 8. Businesswomen—United States—Biography. 9. Legislators—Texas—Biography. 10. Newspaper editors—United States—Biography.
I. Title.
    E840.8.C46W45 2014
    352.2'93092—dc23
    [B]   2013042478

★

To my parents,

Ruthe Lewin Winegarten and Alvin Winegarten,

who encouraged me to live my dreams.

Contents

★

Introduction
ix

CHAPTER ONE
Growing up in Killeen, Texas
1

CHAPTER TWO
Politics and the Texas Legislature: Parliamentarian
11

CHAPTER THREE
Marriage and Family
17

CHAPTER FOUR
Oveta Joins the Army
27

CHAPTER FIVE
The Women's Army Auxiliary Corps
33

CHAPTER SIX
The Little Colonel
43

CHAPTER SEVEN

Running the *Houston Post*

53

CHAPTER EIGHT

Mrs. Secretary and the Polio Epidemic

61

CHAPTER NINE

Retirement and Philanthropy

79

CHAPTER TEN

Oveta's Legacy

93

Time Line

97

Notes

113

Glossary

121

Selected Websites and Resources

127

Selected Bibliography

131

Index

139

Introduction

★

Writing a biography, the story of another person's life, is a tricky undertaking. People are busy living their lives and few take the time to chronicle them as they go. Oveta Culp Hobby worked in the newspaper business a long time. She spent much of her life telling other people's stories, not her own.

I used a variety of sources to compile this account of Oveta's life. I interviewed her son and two of her granddaughters. I read several books that contained information about her, which you can find listed in the bibliography. I read many newspaper articles written about her, especially during her time as director of the Women's Army Corps and secretary of the Department of Health, Education, and Welfare. I consulted her archives, which are collections of her papers, located both at the Woodson Research Center Special Collections Archives at Rice University in Houston, Texas, and the Oveta Culp Hobby Memorial Library at Central Texas College in Killeen, Texas. I also read academic papers and dissertations written about her.

There are many people to whom I owe a debt of gratitude for believing in me and in this project. First is Theresa May, editor-in-chief at the University of Texas Press. Not only did she love this project from the first time I shared it with her, she stood by me as life bounced me around a bit and reminded me to always follow my passions and ideals. My mother, Ruthe Winegarten, instilled in me the love of good storytelling. While most people my age talk of falling asleep at night to the sound of their mothers' sewing machines, my comforting nighttime sound was the rhythmic music of my mother's bright blue IBM Selectric typewriter, which lulled me to sleep as she wrote her books on Texas women's history.

My father, Al Winegarten, always listens to my ideas and still sends me extra money so I can pay for all the little hidden necessities a book like this requires, like photo permissions, so the gorgeous pictures here can bring Oveta's story to life. To my heart partner, Cindy Huyser, who picks up the household duties when I'm immersed in finishing a project, I am always and forever thankful for your support. And to my brother, Marc Sanders, who reminds me not to take myself too seriously and to cherish all the little things in life.

A good writer has good writer friends to read manuscripts and give honest feedback, and I certainly have my share of good writer friends. Nancy Baker Jones and Robert Pando provided much-needed critical reviews that helped keep my errors to a minimum. To the Hobby family—Bill, Diana, Laura Hobby Beckworth, and Heather Catto Kohout—I am indebted for sharing your personal memories of Oveta. To the marvelous women in my Wednesdivas critique group—Marty McAllister, Mary Day Long, P. J. Pierce, and Jeanne Guy—you will always hold a special place in my heart for your diligence and love. To Kimberly Cockrill, who sat with me for endless hours and helped me finish the book, you are my hero.

I have tried to put together as accurate a story as possible about this remarkable woman, and I'm sure I've made mistakes along the way. I've done my best to paint an honest picture of Oveta, to show her sincerity and love of her country, her dedication to making the world a better place, her humor, and her humanity. If this story inspires just one person to take a risk and try to do something they didn't think themselves capable of, I will consider my job to have been done well. I hope you, dear reader, are that person.

Debra L. Winegarten
AUSTIN, TEXAS

★ **OVETA CULP HOBBY** ★

Colonel Oveta Culp Hobby, director of the Women's Army Corps, circa 1945.
Courtesy Culver Pictures Inc.

CHAPTER ONE

Growing up in Killeen, Texas

Oh, it's the easiest thing in the world.
All you have to do is just *be* equal.
OVETA CULP HOBBY, 1978

Lynn Culp opened her front door and reached out to hug her older sister who was visiting from Washington, D.C. She took one look at her sister and stepped back, aghast. Her big sister was wearing a uniform—a *military* uniform!

"Oveta," Lynn said, looking her over with excitement, "what *are* you?"

"I'm a colonel!" Oveta answered.

In 1943, women did not hold such ranks in the Army. In fact, before the start of World War II, women didn't even serve in the military, except as nurses. But Oveta Culp Hobby had just become the first woman in the United States ever to be appointed a colonel. She was the director of the first women's military organization, called the Women's Army Auxiliary Corps, or WAAC, for short. There was a scarcity of manpower in the United States Army, even though most young men between the ages of twenty-one and thirty-five had been drafted or required to sign up for military duty. So many of the men were needed as soldiers on the battlefields that there weren't enough people to fill the noncombat jobs. Congress passed a bill authorizing women to join the military, and Oveta was tapped to lead that effort.

Lynn began to weep when she realized what an important role Oveta had been given.

"Don't cry," Oveta said, comforting her little sister. "I'm going to be the best colonel you've ever seen!"[1]

Shortly thereafter, Lynn, Oveta, and Oveta's husband, William P. Hobby, a former Texas governor, arrived at the Houston Country Club for lunch. They walked into a huge, noisy dining room filled with people but had to wait a few moments for their table. Suddenly, the room became very quiet as people caught sight of Oveta in her new uniform. A few people stood up and started applauding. Soon, everyone in the entire restaurant was standing up, congratulating America's newest and first-ever female colonel, Oveta Culp Hobby.

Once the Hobbys were seated at their table, people came over to congratulate Oveta—so many that a line formed. Oveta was gracious and spoke to everyone who stopped by.

Her sister Lynn said later, "I don't think she got a bite to eat that day."[2]

Because of her accomplishments, Oveta Culp Hobby's name is now etched in today's Texas and American history books, but her life started out far more humbly.

Oveta was born in Killeen, Texas, a small town fifty miles north of Austin, in Bell County, on January 19, 1905. She was the second of seven children born to Ike W. Culp and Emma Elizabeth Hoover Culp. Emma Culp read the name "Oveta" in a romance novel and liked the sound of it so much, she gave the name to her second daughter. In the Cherokee language, the word "oveta" means "forget." But the young Oveta Culp was destined to be unforgettable.

Oveta's father, Ike, was a lawyer in Killeen and a Texas state legislator whose own father, John Robinson Culp, came to Texas after the Civil War. Her great-grandmother, Rachel Eaton Culp, was a "fearless woman who rode on horseback, dodging Indians in darkness when called to aid the sick."[3]

Emma, Oveta's mother, collected food, clothing, and money from the more well-to-do folks in town and shared these resources with the town's poor people. Emma sent Oveta and her sister to deliver baskets of food and clothing to their neighbors who were going through hard times.

★　★　★

Years later, Oveta's sister Lynn asked their mother what Oveta had been like when she was young. To which Emma replied, "Oh, Oveta was never young."[4]

During one church Sunday school class in 1910, the five-year-old Oveta received an unusual assignment.

"Class," her teacher said, "today we're signing pledges for temperance. Each of you will sign your name to this paper. In return, you'll get one of these lovely white ribbons provided by the Woman's Christian Temperance Union."

When it was Oveta's turn to sign the pledge, she looked the paper over, thought about it, and handed the pledge back to her teacher, unsigned.

"Sign your name, Oveta," the teacher said.

"No, ma'am," the young Oveta said politely.

The shocked teacher said, "Oveta, you obey me, or I'm going to tell your mother."

Oveta turned and silently walked back to her desk, waiting for class to be over.

But by the time Oveta got home, her grandmother, who took care of her after school, had received word about the matter. As was often the practice in those days, Grandma had a switch ready, hoping to "beat some sense" into Oveta's five-year-old head. It was only *after* the whipping that Grandma sat Oveta down and asked her why she refused to sign the Sunday school pledge.

Through her tears, Oveta whispered, "I didn't sign because I don't know what temperance means."[5]

Temperance was a social movement that urged banning the sale and drinking of alcoholic beverages. People who promoted the temperance idea pressured the United States government to pass anti-alcohol legislation and encouraged the people in community churches to support their mission. But Oveta didn't know about any of that, and she wasn't willing to sign her name to something she didn't understand.

Oveta's grandmother apologized.

Years later, Oveta told a little more of that story, explaining, "While it's true I didn't know what temperance was, I didn't want to sign the pledge because while I was pretty sure it was something I wouldn't do now, I wasn't sure I might not want to do it in the future, and I didn't want to make a promise on something I wasn't sure I could keep."

Her sister Juanita remembered the day Oveta tried to convince their mother to take her to the movies. Her mother told Oveta no. "If you don't take me," Oveta pouted, "I will throw myself out of the window!" Mrs. Culp told her daughter she had too much to do and was sorry, but she couldn't take her to the movies. Oveta then went to the window ledge, stood on a chair, and hurled herself out the window.

Fortunately, the open windowsill was only about two feet off the ground and, landing in the soft grass, Oveta wasn't hurt in the least.[6]

After the school day was over, rather than going home, Oveta often went to her father's law office, where she spent many afternoons listening to legal talk and reading books far beyond her years or vocabulary. By the time she was ten, she had read the *Congressional Record*, an extraordinary feat for anyone, let alone someone that young.

"Living in a small town as I did," Oveta would later recall, "I guess the *Congressional Record* was sort of spectacular in that it had very broad horizons. . . . It touched all parts of the world, all kinds of issues, and it was an interesting document."[7]

✶   ✶   ✶

Oveta was raised in a prosperous household with six other brothers and sisters, but all the children helped with the family chores. The Culp children picked cotton in the fields. Rich or poor didn't matter in their community; everyone picked their share of cotton.

At the beginning of sixth grade, Oveta's teacher announced to the class that a new Bible would be given to the student with the highest grades in spelling at the end of the school year. Being a lover of both the Bible and reading, Oveta told her teacher, "You might as well put my name on that Bible right now."[8] She was determined to be the winner, and she consistently studied hard all year. By the end of the school year, her teacher awarded Oveta the new Bible, which she later read in full three times.[9]

In the early part of the twentieth century, when Oveta grew up, women were not allowed to vote like men. Every day was full of rigorous chores, both inside the house and out on the farm or ranch. Some women held paid jobs outside the home, but most did not.

In 1917, Texas Governor Jim Ferguson was impeached for, among other things, embezzling state funds. The lieutenant governor, William Hobby, replaced Ferguson and became the youngest person, at age thirty-nine, ever to be governor of

Texas. When election time came around again, Hobby decided to run to keep his governorship, and Mrs. Culp and a great many other women in their rural community decided to help him campaign.

One hot summer afternoon, Oveta's mother stood in their Killeen home doorway. "I can see her open the screen door, and I remember exactly what she had on," Oveta said. "She was wearing a pale blue suit and a white straw hat and high, laced white boots. She was pulling on her gloves, and she turned to my sister and me and said, 'Girls, you'll have to look after the peaches. I'm going out to campaign for Will Hobby.'"[10]

"We had an enormous orchard with peaches, plums, and pears," Oveta remembered. "I spent weeks canning fruit in 1918 while my mother went out campaigning for William Hobby in his race for governor. That was the first year [Texas] women were voting. Hobby had gotten that bill through the legislature so women could vote that year. . . .[11] My mother and a great many other women I knew were really out in the backwoods, looking for votes for him."[12]

In 1918, Governor Hobby defeated Jim Ferguson by the largest majority ever received in a Democratic primary.[13] In Texas, each political party holds what is called a "primary" election, where voters choose which candidates will run for their party in the statewide general election. Little did Oveta know at the time the importance Governor Hobby would play in her life.

In 1919, when Oveta was fourteen years old, the Culp family moved about twenty-five miles east, to Temple, Texas, which was a larger town than Killeen. That same year, Ike Culp was elected as a member to the Texas House of Representatives. Oveta had inherited her father's passion for politics. He frequently took her with him to the Texas state capitol in Austin when the legislature was in session. There, Oveta became a serious observer

Governor William Pettus Hobby, signing the bill giving Texas women the right to vote in primary elections. February 5, 1918. *Austin History Center, Austin Public Library.*

of each day's proceedings and acquired a deeper love for the law and the intricate workings of government.

Ike Culp urged his daughter to get out of their small town as soon as she was able. He understood how much Oveta could offer to the world, and did everything in his power to ensure that she had opportunities to expand her horizons. "My father expected a lot of me," she said. "He was the one who always kept after me to do my best. Certainly my mother and father didn't categorize what was for a girl and what was for a boy to do."[14]

The way the Texas legislature works is that the lawmakers meet from January until May once every two years, and then go back to their homes and maintain their "regular" jobs outside of being state legislators. Because she accompanied her father frequently on his legislative trips to Austin, Oveta had the opportunity to visit the halls of government where her father worked and experience the legislative process in a way most teenagers never do.

Oveta attended Temple High School and did well enough in her classes, but because of her advanced knowledge and experience with the state legislature, she soon became bored with high school. There just wasn't enough intellectual stimulation in the classroom, compared to the excitement of the legislature and law. By the time she was sixteen, she had missed a lot of school because of her frequent trips to Austin with her father.

While in high school, Oveta studied drama and elocution, the art of clear speaking with correct enunciation. She and her friends often put on theater performances for the whole town. She once performed *Alaska, the Brave Cowgirl* so eloquently that a visiting Chautauqua manager offered her a touring position. When her parents refused to let her go, she and her friends formed a group they called "The Jolly Entertainers." They visited nearby towns and raised money to buy church organs.

Oveta's youngest sister, Lynn Culp Loving, told this story relating why Oveta never graduated high school:

> Before graduation, Oveta had a misunderstanding with the principal at Temple High School. She was to prepare and deliver a speech, and the principal read it beforehand and he did not approve of it at all. He told her to write another speech on a different topic.
>
> Oveta was angry. She walked out of Temple High School. Daddy sent her to Baylor Academy, a part of Mary Hardin-Baylor College, at Belton, eight miles from Temple.[15]

It was not unusual for the Culps to entertain Texas politicians and hopeful candidates at their dinner table. The men would jokingly ask Oveta, "Going to be a lawyer like your Daddy when you grow up?" Or, "Gonna run for the legislature in your Pa's place next term?" While the men may have been joking, Oveta took their questions seriously, and she envisioned a legal career of her own some day.

Meanwhile, on August 26, 1920, the Nineteenth Amendment to the United States Constitution became law, giving all women the right to vote, thanks to the efforts of the women's suffrage movement and people like William Hobby. For the first time in American history, women could vote in the full elections, including the presidential elections. This was a groundbreaking time for American women, and by her actions in the movement to grant equality to women, Oveta's mother taught her about standing up for women's rights in our country.

Oveta Culp as parliamentarian of the Texas legislature. *Photo* © Houston Chronicle.

CHAPTER TWO

Politics and the Texas Legislature
Parliamentarian

> If I hadn't been parliamentarian of the Texas Legislature, other things would never have been sparked. Twenty is a wonderful age for things to be sparked.
>
> OVETA CULP HOBBY

A state legislature is a government group whose members discuss and plan policies they think will help the people in their state live better lives. This assembly can pass, amend, and repeal laws. In Texas, the legislature meets for almost five months, once every two years in every odd-numbered year, to write new laws and find solutions to the problems facing the state. The regular session normally lasts 140 days. The governor of Texas can also direct the legislature to meet at other times. These extra meetings are called "special sessions" and can last no more than 30 days. The special sessions deal only with issues chosen by the governor.

Over the many years Oveta accompanied her father to the Texas legislature, she learned about parliamentary procedure. Parliamentary procedure, also known as "rules of order," is the body of rules many different types of organizations follow that helps them make collective decisions in a fair manner. These rules tell the order in which people are allowed to speak, and also how proposals, called bills, are brought before the group for discussion and voting.

These rules are necessary to help keep the actions flowing in a civilized manner, without outbreaks of yelling, arguments, and fighting. Like a game of chess, which has certain rules one must follow to win, parliamentary procedure outlines the rules that a group must follow to reach a decision together. Organizations follow parliamentary procedure to debate and reach group decisions—usually by a vote—with the least possible friction. Because people might have strong differing opinions about the same topic, the rules of order make it possible for everyone to be fairly heard and the issues given an impartial hearing. Parliamentary procedures are the rules governing the game of politics.

Oveta attended Mary Hardin-Baylor College for one year before moving to Austin. By the age of eighteen, Oveta became even busier. She often took advantage of opportunities to learn new things. For instance, she taught school for a short time in Rogers, Texas. She still read law in her father's office and accompanied him to the House of Representatives, but during the summer vacation, she worked in the circulation department of the *Houston Post*. The *Houston Post* was a large newspaper that was to later play a pivotal role in her life.

After her summer stint at the newspaper in Houston, Oveta accepted a position as a staff person in the governor's campaign headquarters of Dan Moody. Dan Moody was the Texas attorney general at the time, and he would be elected governor of Texas in 1926. While serving in Moody's campaign headquarters, Oveta had a firsthand look at the elections process and political campaigns. All these activities laid the groundwork for her future.

Soon, she announced her intention to attend the University of Texas to study law. And attend classes at the University of Texas Law School she did, but Oveta wasn't allowed to officially enroll, because the law school didn't allow women in their formal curriculum.

Meanwhile, back at the state legislature, the parliamentarian, the person responsible for ensuring that proper rules are followed by the state legislators during their meetings, was unable to perform his duties during a special session because of classes he needed to attend at the University of Texas. Oveta, due to her extensive knowledge of and exposure to the many legislative sessions at the Austin capitol, was appointed to take his place. In fact, Oveta was one year shy of the legal voting age, twenty-one, when she received word that she would be selected for the permanent parliamentarian position. By the time the House voted on her nomination later in the year, she had turned twenty-one. It was Oveta's job to make sure the politicians followed proper procedures in debating and voting on public matters. She sat next to the speaker of the house at the head of the room.

This appointment began Oveta's long career as parliamentarian of the Texas legislature. By the end of her tenure, Oveta had served as the parliamentarian in four regular sessions and eleven special sessions of the Texas legislature, under four different speakers of the house. She was the first woman ever to hold the distinguished position as parliamentarian in the Texas House of Representatives. Little did she know at the time that she was destined to be the first woman in other, bigger roles later in her life.

Oveta's role as parliamentarian brought her to the attention of many Texas politicians of the day. Because the legislature typically ran from January until May, every other year Oveta had to find other work to support herself. She moved back to Houston in 1928 and worked as the secretary of the Democratic Club to help plan the National Democratic Convention to be held in Houston later that year. Oveta said she was only a "flunky" in that job, doing everything nobody else wanted to do.[1] However, she did more than that. She sat in on the convention and drank in every word she heard.

Oveta then held a series of positions, among them working on Tom Connally's U.S. senatorial campaign, as well as on a Houston mayoral campaign. In these roles she learned the inner workings of political campaigning and running for office as an elected official.

In October 1929, the stock market crashed, starting a time in U.S. history known as the Great Depression. This period was characterized by high unemployment. Between legislative sessions, Oveta had landed a job as a clerk for the Texas Banking Commission. One of the outcomes of the Great Depression was that many banks failed. Not enough people were repaying their loans because they were out of work, so the banks could not keep the required amount of money on hand to remain solvent.

There was a serious lack of bank examiners to help deal with all the failing banks. One day, the banking commissioner said to Oveta, "Miss Culp, I want you to examine a bank in Temple."

"But commissioner," she replied. "I'm not a bank examiner."

"You are now," said the commissioner, and off Oveta went to Temple.[2] By the time she ended her employment with the State Banking Commission, she had catalogued the entire code of banking laws for the state of Texas.

Oveta's next political work was in Jim Young's campaign for governor. Jim Young was an old friend of the Culp family. This position took Oveta to Dallas, where she met other young women who were also interested in politics. Among them was a young attorney by the name of Sarah T. Hughes, who encouraged Oveta to run for the legislature. Sarah T. Hughes then ran for and served several terms as a district judge in Dallas County. Even though Jim Young's campaign for governor ended in defeat, Oveta's friends in Houston urged her to return to Houston and run for a legislative position in Harris County.[3]

When Oveta was twenty-five, she did run for a seat in the Texas legislature, position number 5 from Harris County. The primary election was held July 26, 1930, and Oveta ran her race as a Democrat. Her campaign faced several obstacles. She was young and not well known in Houston, and Harris County had never named a woman to a state office. Her work in Jim Young's losing campaign proved a handicap, as well. Her opponent managed to defeat her by labeling her both a "Unitarian and a *parliamentarian*."

The word "parliamentarian" was perhaps misunderstood by most voters, and Oveta's opponent made it sound very dark and sinister. He suggested that no right-thinking man or woman would want anyone like that to represent him in the legislature.[4] Unfortunately, the majority of the voters were influenced in a negative way by the political name-calling, and Oveta was defeated.

Oveta was too honest to say she didn't mind the defeat. She did. It was the first real setback she had met, and it dismayed her. Though it was the first and last time she ever ran for public office, she made many friends, both personal and political, who served her well in the future.

The Hobby family: Bill Hobby, Jessica Hobby, Oveta Culp Hobby, William Pettus Hobby. *Courtesy Bill Hobby.*

CHAPTER THREE

Marriage and Family

Everything that ever happened to me fell
in my lap, and nothing in my life would
have been possible without Governor.

OVETA CULP HOBBY

In 1930, after losing her political campaign by only four thousand votes, Oveta resumed her work as assistant to Houston's city attorney. She advised lawyers, wrote opinions, and drafted ordinances.

She then joined the *Houston Post-Dispatch* newspaper as assistant to a cartoonist, and soon transferred to the circulation department.[1] While at the *Post-Dispatch*, she met and maintained a casual friendship—always in groups—with her father's old friend, the former Governor William Pettus Hobby.

Governor Hobby had served two terms as governor of Texas, and Oveta's mother had campaigned for him. After his governorship, he became a successful businessman and the president of the *Houston Post-Dispatch*.[2] Oveta remembered Governor Hobby from the time she was in Austin with her father. He was a fifty-three-year-old widower, whose wife had died from a stroke two years before, in 1928. When Oveta visited Governor Hobby's family in Dallas, she began to realize he was courting her.

Returning to Austin, Oveta was elected state president of the

League of Women Voters.[3] She also served as parliamentarian for another session of the House of Representatives. Meanwhile, she and Governor Hobby continued to see each other, and they soon decided to get married.[4]

Oveta had promised to stay on at the legislature until the session closed. She planned to remain in Austin and marry after the legislative session ended. Some of Governor Hobby's old-fashioned friends advised against this, calling it a "Hollywood marriage."

In what was known as a "gentleman's agreement" between Governor Hobby and the speaker of the House of Representatives, Oveta was effectively discharged from her parliamentarian duties so she could return to Houston as soon as she was married. But she was not told of this agreement until the night before her wedding, after everyone had already committed (she to Governor Hobby and the House speaker to a new parliamentarian). Since the men did this behind her back, the situation came as an unpleasant surprise to Oveta when she heard about it. She thought it a tricky prank, though she made the best of it at the time.[5]

On February 23, 1931, a Monday afternoon, Oveta Culp and Governor William Hobby wed in her parents' Temple, Texas, home. Oveta was twenty-six years old and her husband was twice her age, fifty-three.

Oveta's father, Ike Culp, is said to have told Governor Hobby, "Will, she is going to embarrass you. She doesn't give a hang about clothes and doesn't dress the way she should."[6] By all other accounts, Ike approved of the marriage. Oveta was always more concerned with intellectual pursuits than fashion, never bothering to chase after the latest fashion ideas or trends. During the ceremony, she carried the point-lace handkerchief that her grandmother and sister had also carried down the aisle at their own weddings. Afterward, the couple took a short honeymoon to points in Texas.[7]

Oveta and Governor, as she liked to call her husband, made their home in Houston. Governor restored the *Houston Post-Dispatch* to its original name, the *Houston Post*, and Oveta went to work there learning the newspaper business, first as a research editor and then as a book editor.[8] She thought of herself as assistant to the editor and publisher—her husband.[9]

Oveta first met Lyndon Baines Johnson (LBJ) in the offices of the *Houston Post*, when as a young congressman he had come to meet with Governor Hobby and ask his advice. After Johnson left the governor's office, Will told Oveta, "That's a young man to watch. He will go far."[10] And go far he did, eventually all the way to the White House and the presidency of the United States.

On January 19, 1932, Oveta gave birth to their first child via Caesarean section, a surgical procedure by which an incision is made in the mother's abdomen and the baby is removed through her belly. They named their son William Pettus Hobby, Jr. He was born on Oveta's twenty-seventh birthday.[11]

The governor was delighted with his new eight-and-a-half-pound son, and was quoted several times as saying, "I had no idea babies were so popular, or I would have had them in my platform."[12] This was a joke: a platform consists of the items a politician promises to bring to fruition after a campaign.

Following her son's birth, Oveta returned to work at the newspaper, doing research in the executive department. Shortly afterward, she wrote editorials, produced articles on community issues, and became the literary editor in charge of the Sunday book page. Typical of Oveta Culp Hobby, she didn't stop there. She became involved in a number of committees and boards, like Houston's Museum of Fine Arts, the Junior League, and the Houston Symphony Orchestra Committee. She became the regional chair of the Depression-era-born group Mobilization for Human Needs, and she was the sole female member on a citizens' committee that planned a flood control program for Houston in 1935–1937.

On June 12, 1936, Oveta and Governor took a trip to Dallas to hear President Franklin D. Roosevelt give a speech. On the way back to Houston, flying at an altitude of seven thousand feet, the pilots of their private plane smelled gas and discovered a fire in the oil line. Edwin Hefley, the pilot, threw the plane into a nosedive as flames leaped into the cockpit.

Running into the main cabin, the copilot Eugene Schacher yelled to the four passengers, "Put on your seat belts! We're going to have to land this thing in a hurry!"

Schacher raced back to the cockpit, bracing himself against the seats as the plane plunged almost vertically earthward. Seconds later, he and the pilot burst from the cockpit, flames licking at their heels. But they had to go back in to land the plane.

Reaching through the fire, the pilot thrust his arms into the cockpit and grabbed the control sticks so he could maneuver the plane safely to the ground. But he was too far away from the controls to properly land the plane. Defying death, the pilot climbed back into the fiery cockpit. The copilot was right behind him, attempting to put out the fire as the pilot landed the plane. Nearing the ground, Hefley pulled the plane's nose up as it approached a farmer's plowed cotton field. They were only about twenty miles out of Dallas when they crash-landed in the field. They hit so hard, the landing gear tore off the bottom of the plane.

The passengers pulled the pilot and copilot out of the plane and away from the burning mass of metal. Governor Hobby was knocked unconscious in the crash, and Oveta had to pull him from the plane—no easy feat for a petite woman. Because a lot of fuel remained in the plane's wings, once the fire hit those sections, the plane ignited into a blazing inferno.

The copilot who had fought the flames was badly burned.

Oveta commandeered a dilapidated old car that belonged to Mexican field-workers and drove the injured men to a nearby town where a physician administered first aid.

There, Oveta continued to help care for the injured. She even helped the doctor cut charred clothing from the badly burned pilot and accompanied him in the ambulance to a Dallas hospital. She was so calm throughout the aftermath of the horrible event that it never occurred to the doctor or the hospital attendants that Oveta, too, had been a passenger in the plane when it crashed.

She survived the experience with iron nerves and would allow no one to do anything for her. But as soon as the doctors realized she, too, had been a passenger in the plane, they promptly hospitalized her.[13] Few of those who saw Oveta's calmness that day knew that she was two months pregnant.[14]

Hefley, the pilot, survived the crash, although he spent three months recovering in the hospital. His copilot, Schacher, unexpectedly died the day after the crash due to smoke inhalation and lung damage.

Because they had been in a hurry to return to Houston, the trip was the first time Oveta and the governor broke their pact to never ride in a plane together at the same time. From then on, they honored that agreement.

In true Oveta Culp Hobby fashion, she returned home from the accident and reported for work within a few days. She wanted to write a handbook on parliamentary law and decided to do it that summer. She had been writing a daily newspaper feature on parliamentary law, and her readers indicated to her great interest in the subject on the part of clubwomen, as well as high school and college students. Moving her office to the first floor of the newspaper's building, Oveta wrote her book while continuing her executive and literary editor duties at the *Houston Post*. The book was called *Mr. Chairman*.

On January 19, 1937, Jessica Hobby, Oveta's second child, was born, also via Caesarean section. Her daughter arrived on Oveta's thirty-second birthday.[15]

Caesarean procedures are usually done when a normal childbirth would risk either the baby or the mother's life. But because of the timing of the children's births, both on Oveta's birthday, many years later one of Oveta's granddaughters suggested that her grandmother actually chose for her children to share her birthday.

A few months after Jessica's birth, Oveta went horseback riding in the park. The horse was skittish and, while cantering, threw Oveta off. The fall broke Oveta's leg and shattered a wrist. But being laid up didn't stop her! She edited the Sunday book page from her bed and continued a research study she had started for the *Post*. As soon as she was able, she returned to the office on crutches and resumed her newspaper work.[16]

Also in 1937, Oveta was elected a member of the American Society of Newspaper Editors—only the second female in the history of its membership. She was chair of the Speakers' Bureau for the first Women's Crusade (Community Chest work) and chair of the Crusade itself for two consecutive years. In November of 1937, she was appointed the Texas chair of the Advisory Committee on Women's Participation for the 1939 New York World's Fair.

Meanwhile, her book *Mr. Chairman* was published by the Economy Company in 1936, and in October 1938 was adopted as a textbook for Texas public schools.

In 1938, Oveta was named executive vice president of the *Houston Post*. Under her direction, the newspaper began covering events important to Houston's black community and featuring blacks in newspaper stories.[17]

In 1939, for about $4 million, the Hobbys bought the *Houston Post* from Houston financier Jesse Jones, who also owned the rival newspaper, the *Houston Chronicle*.[18] Oveta and Governor worked hard together to pay off this large debt.

Over time, the couple made a number of other business decisions that grew their family wealth. One of them was the purchase of their first television station, KLEE, which later became KPRC.

Oveta had been sitting in her office when her phone rang. It was Judge Elkins calling.

"I want you to see W. Albert Lee," he said.

"Why?"

"Because he owns KLEE and he wants to sell half his interest."

At the time, KLEE was Houston's only television station. The Hobbys had an application in with the Federal Communications Commission (FCC) for a broadcasting channel, but at the time the FCC had frozen all the applications pending the results of a survey.

"So, how much money is he losing?" Oveta asked.

"Lots," the judge said.

Shortly after their conversation, Mr. Lee came to see Oveta, at Judge Elkins's suggestion.

"I haven't seen your financials, of course," Oveta said to him, "but I understand that you are losing money on a regular basis."

Lee said he had to have a cancer operation on his leg and felt he needed to partner with someone who knew how to run a TV station. He wanted to sell half his interest in the station. In reality, television was so new at the time that there weren't many who knew anything about running a station. And so far, all the Hobbys' experience lay in newspapers and radio.

When Oveta later recounted the meeting to Judge Elkins, he said, "Why don't you buy 100 percent?"

"Because," she replied, "I don't have the money to buy it, and I don't have the money to lose."

The judge kept after Oveta to buy KLEE until she finally said, "Can I borrow the money from you?"

"Yes."

Oveta knew television was an unknown field but felt it held great promise. She and Mr. Lee talked it over and came to the agreement that she would buy half his interest in the station. Then, however, the FCC came out with a ruling saying it would only grant a license to someone owning a controlling interest, which meant 51 percent ownership.

The good Judge Elkins called Oveta again.

"Mr. Lee wants to sell 100 percent, and it's a good investment."

"We don't have the money!" Oveta told him.

"I'll lend you the money," the judge told her.

So Mr. Lee and the Hobbys agreed that the Hobbys would buy the whole station for $745,000. Mr. Lee tried to strike a side deal, asking Oveta, "If I sell you my television station, will you take your clothes to my laundry?" He owned the Walee Laundry.

At the time, the governor had been at Dr. Turner's Neurological Center for six months being treated for another illness, often near death. Oveta told him the whole plan. They could see the dangers, but they wanted a TV station and had no way of knowing when the FCC might lift its freeze on granting new licenses.

The governor told Oveta, "I will rely on your judgment."

Since televisions were just being developed, TV sets were expensive, and only the wealthy could afford them. Television producers were just starting to figure out what types of programs would be popular and how to make money from them. Because the industry was so speculative, Oveta called her good friend, Senator Lyndon Baines Johnson. Senator Johnson's wife, Lady Bird, owned a television station in Austin. Oveta asked what he thought about the future of TV. Senator Johnson told her he "thought it would go through some rough days, but the future was very bright."[19]

Oveta was convinced that buying the station was the right thing to do. She just wasn't sure they could afford it. Still, she attended the meeting, with Judge Elkins there to represent her. The judge put a check down in front of her to sign, and she whispered to him, "You know this check will bounce, don't you?"

Judge Elkins didn't bat an eye. He said very quietly, "I have other papers for you to sign, and by the time this check gets to the bank, the money will be in your account."

When Oveta got back to the *Post*, she told her chief financial officer what she had done.

He climbed one hundred walls straight up. "You don't have the authority to sign such a check!" he said.

"I know," Oveta said, "but I've done it."

"According to the bylaws, there have to be TWO signatures," he said. "Does the governor know about this?"

Oveta nodded. "In detail."

But having signed, Oveta had to tell George Butler, who was on her board of directors and who *should* have been notified of the signing before it happened.

George was beside himself. By this time, Oveta had brought Governor home to convalesce. George called her and said, "I feel that I must register my disapproval."

"Fine. Come tomorrow and tell Governor, and then stay for lunch with me," Oveta replied.

On Friday, George came by. Oveta insisted that he see Governor alone so he would not modify his disapproval because of her presence. When George came downstairs after seeing Governor, he told Oveta, "Governor said that you now have the responsibility of running things, and 'I've never doubted her judgment before. I shan't start now.'"

When Mr. Lee died, Judge Elkins escorted Oveta to the funeral. He leaned over and murmured, "And you never *did* take him your laundry."[20]

While the Hobbys were in the early stages of building their personal fortunes, across the ocean things were getting dire. Germany had invaded Poland, and two days later, on September 3, 1939, France and Britain declared war on Germany. This marked the beginning of World War II.

At the time, the top military brass had gone to Congress asking for a peacetime draft in an attempt to increase the number of enlisted men in the military. Although the United States had not yet joined the war effort, military leaders could see it was only a matter of time before the U.S. would need to get involved. As a result of the draft, the War Department started receiving thousands of letters a day from women all over the country, wanting to know what, exactly, the government would be doing with their sons and brothers who were being forced into military service.

In response, the White House created the Women's Interest Section in the War Department's Bureau of Public Relations. General Surles, the director of public relations for the Army, had been searching for a woman who was willing to come in and set up this bureau.

Oveta happened to be in Washington, D.C., attending a Federal Communications Commission (FCC) meeting on KPRC business, the radio station that she and the governor owned. General Surles invited her to take the job of running the bureau, where she would to try to communicate to women across the country the necessity of the peacetime draft and explain the types of training the men had to have.[21]

Oveta refused the offer, explaining that she had a husband, two small children, and a full-time job with the *Houston Post*.[22]

CHAPTER FOUR

Oveta Joins the Army

My father taught me that I could turn the world
around just as well as any of my brothers.

OVETA CULP HOBBY

The telephone blared in the Houston home of Oveta and Governor William Hobby. Oveta wondered who would call during the nice evening meal. With the family's busy lives, Sunday dinner was one of the few times they had to be together. She threw down her napkin and went to answer the phone. She listened to the caller and said a few words the family couldn't quite hear from the dinner table. At the call's end, she returned to the table.

"What was that all about?" the governor asked his wife.

"That was General Surles," she replied. "He called again to ask me to come to Washington and head up this new women's army organization he's putting together."

"He called *again*? Do you mean this isn't the first time he's called about this?"

"Heavens, no. He asked me last week, and I turned him down. I told him there was no possible way I could do such a thing, not with my responsibilities to you and the children and the newspaper. I told him he would just have to find someone else. I'm not interested in that job."

"I can't believe you made him ask you twice," the governor told Oveta. "You must do whatever your country asks you to do. You shouldn't have made him ask you a second time. Any thoughtful person knows that we are *in* this war, and that every one of us is going to have to do whatever we are called upon to do."[1]

Oveta knew he was right. She called General Surles back and agreed to take the new job on a six-month basis; she felt like she couldn't afford to be away from the newspaper and her young family for a longer period of time. The job was in Washington, D.C. Oveta would be paid one dollar per year for her services.

Before Oveta set off for Washington, the governor called her sister Lynn and asked her to take Oveta to lunch and then go buy some new clothes, but to do so without letting on that the whole thing was the governor's idea. Lynn took Oveta to lunch at the old Houston Club, downtown, and then told her older sister, "I'm going to go across the street to Ben Wold's Fashion, and I wish you'd go with me."

Once Lynn got Oveta into the dressing room, she said that Oveta was "*lost*, almost like a child. It was charming. We were there trying on dresses until the store closed at 7. Oveta just couldn't make up her mind which ones to choose." Growing up, Oveta's passion had been focused on books, not fashion, and she really didn't know what to do.

Lynn said, "Let's take these seven or eight dresses home and give Governor a fashion show." When they got home, the governor wore a huge smile as Oveta modeled the dresses for him. She ended up keeping them all. A few days later, the governor caught Lynn alone and told her, "You sure did teach her well."[2]

In June 1941, thirty-six-year-old Oveta Hobby arrived in Washington, D.C. She got right to work and began the formidable task of setting up the new Women's Interest Section of the War Department's Bureau of Public Relations. One of her main jobs was to prove to American mothers that the Army provided for the welfare of their sons.[3]

"For every one of the 1,500,000 men in the Army today," she said in an early interview, "there are four or five women— mothers, wives, sisters, sweethearts—who are closely and personally interested."[4] Oveta soon became a pen pal "to thousands of wives and sweethearts all over the country, assuring them the Army was taking good care of their men. One of the most frequent questions she got was, 'How is the food?' She smoothly answered, 'It's getting better all the time.'"[5]

As if she didn't have enough to do as head of the Women's Interest Section, General Marshall then asked Oveta to plan our nation's first women's army, which would eventually be called the Women's Army Auxiliary Corps. Oveta studied the British and French women's armies and prepared a plan by which the United States could avoid making the same mistakes the Europeans had.

Once the plan was complete and submitted to General Marshall, Oveta was released to go home for the winter holidays. On Sunday, December 7, 1941, her flight to Houston included a detour to Chicago, Illinois, so she could give a speech to the American Farm Federation Convention on the subject of women's roles in the not-yet-begun war.[6] Getting off the airplane, reporters met her with the news that the Japanese had just bombed Pearl Harbor, Hawaii.

Oveta went ahead with her speech, which was inspired; General Marshall later said, "Oveta Hobby made the nation's first declaration of war that day."[7]

The speech done, Oveta rushed to the telephone and called her husband. "Governor, the Japanese have just bombed Pearl Harbor, and all hell is breaking loose across the country!"

"Oveta," Governor said, "I know you've had this trip home planned for a while, but your country is more important. I'll take care of this family. You turn around and go back to Washington and do what you need to do."

Oveta hung up the phone, relieved. This was the day she'd anticipated for months, and she knew her place was in Washington, D.C., where she could oversee all the plans and preparations for the women's army that she'd spent the last months developing.

A day later, on December 8, 1941, President Franklin Delano Roosevelt declared war on Japan and officially entered World War II. Three days later, on December 11, Adolf Hitler declared war on the United States on behalf of Germany.

The Japanese raid on Pearl Harbor left the United States with no alternative, and it clarified in Americans' eyes the need for U.S. involvement. World War II escalated in earnest.

Upon Oveta's return to D.C., she was appointed to the pre-planning committee for the new Women's Army Auxiliary Corps.

Seven months before, on May 28, 1941, Congresswoman Edith Nourse Rogers introduced House Resolution 4906 (HR 4906): "A bill to establish a Women's Army Auxiliary Corps for Service with the Army of the United States." But the bill faced much opposition and stalled in Congress. Now, with World War II well underway, the push for the new corps became urgent and intense, and a great legislative fight ensued in pursuit of the bill's passage.

While the War Department worked feverishly on planning for the Women's Army Auxiliary Corps, or WAAC, Secretary of War Henry Stimson and General George Marshall tasked Oveta with figuring out what jobs women could do in regular Army procedures with the least amount of special training. Oveta provided them with a plan and list of duties.

Based on her report, General Marshall sent Oveta to Capitol Hill to testify in front of Congress about how women serving in the WAAC could release men for frontline duty. He also asked Oveta to draw up a list of women who might command this new women's army.[8]

Oveta provided a list of nine possible commanders to General Marshall and Secretary Stimson, and they held the list for quite some time. Congresswoman Rogers, author of the WAAC bill, was also asked to recommend candidates. She submitted one name for consideration: Oveta Culp Hobby.[9]

At this point, Oveta had been with the Public Relations Bureau of the War Department for almost a year, despite the fact that she agreed to take on the job for only six months. Senior officers wrote of Oveta: "She has the ability, vision, and is broad-minded enough to assemble a staff of capable assistants around her. [She is] already known to most of the key people in government and War Department Circles."[10] They noted her personal energy, magnetism, sincerity, and idealism, and observed that a very considerable diplomatic ability on all matters was combined with a certain stubborn determination in pursuing major issues.[11]

The chief of staff informed Secretary of War Stimson that Oveta was his choice for the position of director of the WAAC because of her brilliant work in the Bureau of Public Relations and during negotiations for the WAAC bill. He said, "She has won the complete confidence of the members of the War Department Staff with whom she has come into contact, and she made a most favorable impression before the Committee of Congress."[12]

Finally, General Marshall and Secretary Stimson called

Oveta in to meet with them. When Oveta arrived at General Marshall's office, he read over her list of nine names, then gingerly placed it facedown on his desk.

"Oveta," General Marshall said, "I'd rather you took the job."

"General, I cannot," she told him.

But when Oveta discussed it with her husband, he said she could and should do it. She was caught between the two men she respected most in the world, General Marshall and her husband. She finally decided to accept the position, becoming the first director of the Women's Army Auxiliary Corps. She was thirty-seven years old at the time.

But Oveta found herself in a strange limbo. She was the unannounced head of a nonexistent office, which could not become WAAC headquarters until passage of the WAAC legislation at an uncertain future date. Yet she still had to perfect complete plans for the WAAC, which required formal coordination with many War Department agencies.[13]

On May 14, 1942, nearly a year after the WAAC bill was introduced, the Senate approved Public Law 554, which was signed into law the next day by the president of the United States, Franklin Delano Roosevelt, officially creating the first Women's Army Auxiliary Corps.[14] With the stroke of the president's pen, the WAAC came into existence and, with it, Oveta's destiny.

CHAPTER FIVE

The Women's Army Auxiliary Corps

You have taken off silk and put on khaki.
You have a debt and a date.
A debt to democracy, a date with destiny.

OVETA CULP HOBBY

When Oveta Culp Hobby attended her swearing-in ceremony as director of the Women's Army Auxiliary Corps, on May 15, 1942, she was wearing a dress, a fancy hat she had chosen, and white gloves because there was not yet a military uniform for women.[1] Her military career then began in earnest.

On May 27, 1942, the first women could officially enlist in the Women's Army Auxiliary Corps (WAAC). In Washington, D.C., the WAAC headquarters was stormed on recruiting day by 750 candidates, over three times the number anticipated. Twice during the day, officials ran out of application blanks. By the end of the day, 13,208 women from all over the country had filled out applications to join the corps.[2]

In June of 1942, the first WAAC khaki uniform was delivered, specially made for Director Hobby. She put it on and reported to the chief of staff. When she returned to her office, she was wearing a colonel's silver eagles, which he had pinned on and

"I never did learn to salute properly or master the thirty-inch stride," Oveta Culp Hobby said, noting that Army regulations prohibited her from attending officer's training since she was the director of the Women's Army Auxiliary Corps. *Courtesy Corbis Images.*

directed her to wear.[3] She was not officially promoted to the rank of colonel until a year later.

Oveta's job as director of the newly organized WAAC was all-consuming. She traveled constantly, speaking to large audiences of both men and women on the radical subject of the time: enlisting volunteer women in the Army. She traveled with an electric fan and an iron so that at each overnight stop she could wash, dry, and iron her khaki uniform—still the only women's uniform in existence at the time.[4] Director Hobby soon enlisted the help of well-known designers to make a WAAC uniform that would be attractive to large numbers of young women. However, the Army Quartermaster Corps vetoed the uniform's belt as a waste of leather and the pleats in the skirt as a waste of cloth, so the final WAAC uniform was a variant on the basic design of the Quartermaster Corps' uniform.[5] It was not very attractive. The hat became known as the "Hobby Hat," because the women claimed that Oveta was the only person who actually looked good in it.

The WAACs occupied a unique place in the government—or rather, a *lack* of a place. Because Congress was unwilling to make the women's corps an integral part of the Army, the women in the War Department found themselves in a holding pattern. For instance, when Director Hobby sent requests to Army engineers for plans for WAAC barracks, the engineers replied that they worked only for the Army, and the WAAC was not Army. As a result, Director Hobby and her staff had to draw up their own barracks plan.[6]

Since women had never been in the Army before, each and every contingency had to be addressed. Director Hobby had literally thousands of decisions to make, and very little information with which to make those decisions. Though the WAAC was a military organization, in the beginning it didn't offer Army rank, officer status, equal pay, or Army benefits such as retirement and veteran's rights. These assets wouldn't happen until 1943.[7]

Bringing into being an entire Army Corps is a daunting task, even for trained military professionals. The workload at the WAAC headquarters—never light—suddenly became so great as to seriously threaten efficiency. A fourteen-hour day and a seven-day week became standard in the director's office. Staff members reported that for days at a time, Mrs. Hobby and her assistants worked every night until three, five, and sometimes seven o'clock in the morning. They averaged only two or three hours of sleep each night or merely went home for a quick shower and coffee before returning to work.[8]

Director Hobby and her WAACs suffered many indignities and faced many barriers to the acceptance of their place in the Army. Commanding officers were horrified at the thought of women soldiers. Most Army sergeants had their own jeeps. Although she was a U.S. Army officer, Oveta had to call for a car from the transportation pool.[9] She was also invited to use the facilities of the Army-Navy Club; the club official asked, however, if she would mind coming in by the back door.[10]

On July 20, 1942, 440 chosen women arrived at Fort Des Moines in Iowa to attend the WAAC's first officer candidate class. Oveta herself applied for the school so she could understand through her own experience how a woman adjusted to military training. Her shocked advisors had no luck changing her mind. Finally, General George Marshall told her firmly that such an action was impossible under the Army's system of rank.

"It never would have crossed my mind to command an army of women. I never did learn to salute properly or master the thirty-inch stride," Oveta said.[11] She had been at Fort Des Moines since the first day, observing the women in training somewhat wistfully. On the fourth day of their enlistment, she addressed the ranks of newly minted soldiers.[12]

Despite the WAAC's early recruiting success, their maltreatment by some Army personnel continued. For instance, on the WAAC's first payday, the comptroller general's office decreed that it could not pay the WAAC women doctors. The comptroller was only authorized to pay "persons serving as doctors in the military service, and women are not persons." Secretary of War Stimson had to make a rush trip to Capitol Hill for a special act of Congress to enable Director Hobby to pay her physicians.[13]

Colonel Hobby made sure that even though the troops had to be segregated by race, black women officers led the black women soldiers. Here, she is speaking with Mary McLeod Bethune, who later founded the National Council of Negro Women.
Courtesy Corbis Images.

As a staunch supporter of civil rights, Oveta campaigned to make sure that not only were black women represented in the Women's Army Auxiliary Corps, but that they were also invited to be part of the first class of Corps officers. She wanted to be sure that even though the women were segregated according to race, the black women would have qualified officers of their own race as leaders.[14] When Director Hobby again visited Fort Des Moines in September 1942, she found conditions for the women unacceptable.

Lieutenant Betty Bandel, Director Hobby's aide, wrote about that visit:

It was snowing! As soon as I hit the post, I realized the winter uniforms had not yet been issued—the new companies did not even have their complete summer outfits! And mud and slush was a foot deep . . . Then I discovered there was *no heat* in many barracks. Shortage in metal pipes made it impossible for plumbers to install radiators . . . [T]he mills had fallen down on the clothing deal, and it was impossible to outfit all the kids with winter uniforms.

Incidentally, this is the first time in 67 years snow has fallen in Des Moines in September. It's usually hotter than anything. Friday night I got together with some of the officers, and they thought there were enough pieces of clothing in the warehouses to wrap something around each girl, if you paid no attention to sizes. Saturday morning I reported that to the Colonel, giving her a picture of what I had seen . . . She, with a gleam in her eye, sailed up to Colonel Morgan and asked for an order issuing every piece of warm clothing, no matter what the fit or anything, on a temporary, emergency basis. Even enlisted men's coats, if there were any, were to be issued. By mid-afternoon the kids were getting a coat here, a raincoat there, a sweater in the next place . . . [T]hat is a sample of how the Little Colonel works.[15]

Colonel Hobby had an uncanny ability to garner her troops' support, as Lt. Bandel reported:

Saturday morning, I called the Colonel up and asked her if she wanted to wear wool or khaki to inspect her troops. She said, "What is your thought, Lieutenant? That if most of the women don't have wool, we shouldn't wear it?"
I said, "Well, er—"

She said, "Correct. Summer uniform."

In summer stuff, and the regular light raincoat, she inspected barracks and mess halls—and one hour later it was all over the post that she had done so, and the girls were eating out of her hand. She spoke at graduation—in summer uniform—and personally presented diplomas.[16]

The initial success of the Women's Army Auxiliary Corps depended, in large part, on the ability of Director Hobby and her staff to actually recruit and enlist the thousands of women nationwide needed to fill its ranks and perform the duties required to help support the male troops in the field. Although the recruits had to be trained on every phase of military life, from how to wear the WAAC uniform to marching and saluting, it wasn't long before the women showed their colors and new recruits began enlisting in record numbers.

One of the recruitment tools was a series of promotional films showing the training requirements for becoming a WAAC. Some of these films have been preserved and can be viewed online on YouTube.

- Women's Army Corps, Part I
  http://www.youtube.com/watch?v=ALow_k85n2s&feature=related
- Women's Army Corps, Part 2
  http://www.youtube.com/watch?v=efCMW1qOiks&feature=related
- Women's Army Corps, Part 3 (Contains an officer's graduation speech given by Director Hobby with her famous quote, "A debt to democracy, a date with destiny.")
  http://www.youtube.com/watch?v=XxML6I2JGbo

In October, 1942, Director Hobby and First Lady Eleanor Roosevelt were invited by Queen Elizabeth to visit England and see how the British women were aiding in the war effort.[17] First Lady Eleanor Roosevelt wrote:

> On October 21, [I] appeared at the airport on Long Island at the appointed time, together with Director Oveta Hobby, head of the Women's Army Corps, Lieutenant Betty Bandel, her aide, a courier from the State Department, and Mr. Slater, one of the vice-presidents of the American Export Lines. It was a nonstop flight, one of the first to be made. We were luxuriously taken care of and had only one piece of excitement on the way, when we were allowed to look down on a convoy below us—little tiny specks on the ocean. It was hard to believe that those ships were in danger and that some of them might suddenly be torpedoed. . . .
>
> Our first bad weather was in Foynes, Ireland. We had expected to transfer there from our plane to another and continue on to London; but as we landed on the water, a small boat came out from shore and we were told that our flight to London had been canceled because of weather . . . We climbed out after making sure that our military ladies were *un*military in dress; if they had gone ashore in military uniform they would have been interred because that part of Ireland was neutral.[18]

Lieutenant Bandel, Oveta's aide, described Director Hobby's frustration at the bureaucratic procedures to make things happen. "She has a true newspaperwoman's 24-hour deadline sense, and the way War Department people will take a week or two to make up a plan when some big thing is being held up waiting for it drives her wild. They work thoroughly and well, and she would be the last one to advocate sloppiness or error, but, as she often says, 'We can dot the I's after the war is over.'"[19]

Lieutenant Bandel later wrote, "At Claridge's, we had a suite of a living room and two bedrooms. She was working on a speech at a desk and looked over at me and noticed a button on my jacket was hanging loose. 'Take off that jacket,' she said, and suddenly she realized that *she* was sewing a button on *my* uniform. She pointed a finger at me and declared, 'You're fired!' Fortunately for me, she was kidding."[20]

Despite the challenges, the all-volunteer WAACs quickly showed that one WAAC could often do the work of two men in certain tasks—from secretarial work to PBX operation to kitchen patrol to parachute folding.[21]

Colonel Hobby and Kate Smith sharing a moment after selling World War II war
bonds on Kate Smith's radio show. *Courtesy Culver Pictures.*

CHAPTER SIX

The Little Colonel

We have a common cause, the cause of human decency.
And the harder we work, the fewer lives will be lost.

OVETA CULP HOBBY

Oveta dreaded this moment. Ordering three hundred of her finest troops into a meeting room, she addressed them with her aide, Lieutenant Betty Bandel, standing by her side.

"Women," Oveta said, "today is a glorious day in the history of our Corps. General Eisenhower has asked that I send him three hundred of my finest soldiers. Your officers have nominated each of you for these positions. I will not lie to you. You will be going overseas. You will be serving in combat zones. There's a good chance that you may not come back home again.

"As your commander, it is my duty to inform you of the risks involved if you accept this assignment. Remember, you have no formal military status, and should you be injured or killed, there will be no remuneration for your families.

"I will not order anyone to go. I am asking for volunteers. Knowing the dangers involved, you must go of your own free will. I do not want it on my conscience that I sent even one of you into certain danger against your wishes. The need is great or the General would not have made this request. If you are willing to serve in this capacity, step forward to fill the unit."

Of the three hundred women in the room, 298 instantly volunteered. Seeing this, Director Hobby was unable to continue speaking and hastily sought privacy in a broom closet.[1]

In February 1943, General White of the Army told a Senate committee that, "Wherever we have put the WAAC, they have proved highly valuable." He also told the committee that, in his opinion, "a WAAC unit would not be able to replace an equal number of men. I have always estimated that three women would release two men."[2] By the next month, though, he had to change his tune.

Reports from the first unit at Fort Sam Houston indicated that three women had replaced not two men, but four. It was indicated that one woman could not replace men in heavy work such as motor transport, but that women stenographers, typists, and switchboard operators could often replace "two or more men apiece."[3]

The first WAAC Training Center at Fort Des Moines, Iowa, was bitterly cold on Valentine's Day 1943, when Director Hobby reviewed her troops with First Lady Eleanor Roosevelt.[4]

The women were so competent that it became clear—with a lot of hard work on the parts of Director Hobby and her staff— that women should be admitted into the regular Army. Thereafter, in 1943, the Corps received full Army status. The word "Auxiliary" was dropped from the official name, and the organization became known as the Women's Army Corps, or WAC.

On July 5, 1943, while living in Washington, D.C., Oveta Culp Hobby was promoted to the rank of colonel and director of the Women's Army Corps. With this appointment, she became the first woman colonel in the history of the U.S. military services. Standing a full five feet four inches tall, her staff dubbed her

"The Little Colonel," a name that stuck with her throughout her military career.

★ ★ ★

Lieutenant Betty Bandel, Oveta's aide, wrote her family often to share her travels and adventures. From time to time, Betty's letters provided a glimpse, as well, into the toll that being the head of the Women's Army Corps took on Oveta.

On September 27, 1943, Betty wrote the following letter to her mother:

> Dear Maw,
> The L.C. (Little Colonel), poor lassie, has had a sick husband and child to look after lately. The Governor [came to Washington, D.C.] to have an operation about a week ago, and she was simply worried to death. She spent sleepless nights running out to the hospital to see him, trying to dig up a nurse (they're scarce as hen's teeth today), and getting somebody to look after young Jessica, who went off her feed the way children will when things are upset around them. Add to all this a small apartment, with young William and Jessica in it, and you have some idea of what [is on] that one woman's shoulders, aside from what I consider the most trying job in the War Department.
> I have seen her drag herself together for a hard conference, in which everything hung on the phrasing of an idea's presentation, when she would have to pull herself up out of her chair by holding on to the edge of her desk—and yet when she went into it, five minutes later, with fresh make-up on, no one in the room would have dreamed she was anything but sailing along at the top of her form, full of energy, strength, composure. Don't ever tell any of this to

anyone—she never even tells people in the office of her family obligations, and has almost a fetish for refusing to place herself in a position which would seem to demand sympathy. Which fills me with such sympathy that it is sometimes hard to bear. The other day she told me suddenly of her husband's illness; I started to ask if there was anything I could do, and found myself brought up short by a sudden and wholly unexpected full-grown set of tears in my eyes and throat; she followed suit, at the unexpected sight; and we both began to laugh, ending in near-hysterics.[5]

Lieutenant Bandel also wrote of their next trip to Britain, and about how she and Oveta made their way to Italy and North Africa:

While we were in Cairo, we took time off to see the Pyramids. Oveta got on a camel, Major Wally Burgoyne got on a donkey, and I decided to stay on terra firma. Our WAC skirts were short and fairly tight, and never in this world would I have gotten aboard one of those beasts unless I first had retired behind a Pyramid and put on slacks.[6]

Oveta Culp Hobby's causes were legion, but she didn't let them overwhelm her. When she learned that women were going to be dishonorably discharged for "pregnancy without permission" (i.e., getting pregnant without first being married), she got after the generals. She argued that male soldiers who fathered illegitimate children should, in all fairness, get the same treatment, and suffer the same loss of rights and pay. As a result, the regulations were changed, and the pregnancy without permission cases were thereafter given medical treatment and honorable discharges.[7]

Colonel Hobby posing in front of the Great Pyramid in Giza, Egypt. *Courtesy National Archives, photo no. 111-SC-241144.*

Waging an overseas war was not only costly in terms of people power; it also took a lot of money to subsidize the military operations. The U.S. had suffered the Great Depression from 1929 to 1941, and the government was hard-pressed to pay for these huge new military operations. Franklin D. Roosevelt reinstated the use of the "war bond" as a means of raising money to pay for the ramp-up in military spending. Essentially, a war bond is a loan made to the government. A person could purchase a bond for as little as $18.25 and be repaid $25 by the government ten years later. The idea was that the government needed the money now to help pay for the war and ten years would be a long enough time period for the war to have ended and the economy to have recovered so that the loan could be repaid.

Many celebrities donated their time and energy to raise money for the war effort. One of the greatest fund-raisers was the nationally known singer Kate Smith. Kate had her own one-hour radio show on which she sang Irving Berlin's anthem, "God Bless America."[8] She participated in two radio marathons to sell war bonds. One of the most successful single events was a sixteen-hour marathon radio broadcast on CBS, during which nearly $40 million worth of bonds were sold. Patriotism and the spirit of sacrifice could be expressed with war bond purchases, and millions of Americans jumped aboard the effort.[9] Over the course of World War II, Kate raised $600 million in war bonds.[10]

The Women's Army Corps was riding high on its successes, and by the time General Dwight Eisenhower was in England preparing for D-Day, his call was constant: "Send me more WACs!" By 1944, WAC headquarters had requests from commanding generals around the world for six hundred thousand women—three times the total authorized strength of the corps.[11]

But for Colonel Oveta Hobby, the days, weeks, and months of nonstop traveling and constant stress finally began to impact her well-being. In the summer of 1944, Colonel Hobby took a six-week medical leave to recover from exhaustion and illness.[12]

On January 8, 1945, Secretary of War Henry L. Stimson awarded Oveta the Distinguished Service Medal for outstanding service. She became the first woman in the history of the military to receive the medal.

Her citation read, in part:

Without guidance or precedents in the United States military history to assist her, Colonel Hobby established sound initial policies, planned and supervised the selection of officers and the preparation of regulations. The soundness of basic plans and policies . . . is evidenced by the outstanding success of the Women's Army Corps . . . Her contribution to the war effort of the nation has been of important significance.[13]

Working twelve- to fifteen-hour days continued to take its toll on the forty-year-old colonel. By July 1945, Oveta Culp Hobby was exhausted and ill. She knew she had completed the work she had been asked to do. When she requested permission to resign, on July 12, 1945, she was asked to take her final physical examination at the Pentagon because it would be less noticeable. "If you go to Bethesda," Pentagon officials explained, "we'll be bombarded by people wanting your job for somebody."

Drooping with fatigue, Colonel Hobby walked the long corridor from the driveway ramp to the Pentagon dispensary, not sure she would get there. She emerged with a card certifying that she was fit for overseas duty. On her release, Governor was waiting for her with a stretcher. He took her to the train and directly from Washington to Doctors' Hospital in New York for rest and treatment.[14]

On July 15, 1945, Lt. Betty Bandel wrote her mother about the latest development in Oveta's career:

Well, this week saw the end of an era. Little D-WAC [referring to Oveta, standing for "Little Director, Women's Army Corps] had to do what Jess and I have feared she might have to do at any time for the last 12 months: go home. Her own health has been anything but good for long months, and now various family problems have arisen— business and things. Do not pass this on to anyone, as she does not wish to air her problems to the world. Some brief explanation will probably be made to the members of the Corps, and to the world, this next week. I have never felt so sorry for anyone.

She fought through the battle of wondering whether she should leave, for her own health, six months ago, and had determined to stay on until the end, when suddenly about two or three weeks ago other things came up that made it imperative for her to leave the service. She told only four of us, before the press conference last Wednesday . . . Poor Westray, who has to take over her job, only knew about it three days before it all happened.

Her name has been inextricably linked with the WAC. She . . . began her outfit and worked with it throughout its period of growth. It will be quite something for the public to get used to anyone else as the Director, WAC. But it will mean the final integration of women in the military service.[15]

Oveta almost made it to the end of World War II, which ended on September 2, 1945. She initially identified fifty-four jobs that women were qualified to perform in the Army. By 1945, that original list had expanded to 239 jobs, ranging from riveters, interpreters, balloon-gas chemists, surveyors, and boiler inspectors in such far-flung places as India, North Africa, and Egypt.[16] By April 1945, the WACs had recruited over 99,000 women, with WACs qualifying for 406 of the 628 military occupations.[17]

Oveta Culp Hobby was a woman of great vision and understood the role she and the women of the WAC had played in shaping the course of history for women in America. In an interview in 1980, she said, "I think women working during the war had a tremendous influence on moving women into the labor force—not only those who served in the military, but also those who held jobs in the factories and other war-related jobs. When I went to say goodbye to General Marshall when I left, he said, 'When you're rested, write a memorandum to the file on utilization of women power.' . . . I smiled at him and I said, 'General, I'll write it if you tell me to, but if you need to recruit women in such numbers again, the conditions will be different! You have no idea what is going to happen in the woman power field as a result of this war, because of women in the armed services and in the civilian jobs that they took during the war.'"[18]

Secretary of War Henry L. Stimson congratulates Colonel Oveta Culp Hobby upon winning the Distinguished Service Medal, the Army's third-highest honor. *Courtesy Culver Pictures Inc.*

CHAPTER SEVEN

Running the *Houston Post*

I think I'll like Houston if they ever get it finished.

OVETA CULP HOBBY

Returning to Houston and her job as executive vice president of the *Houston Post* after retiring from being the director of the Women's Army Corps, Oveta walked into a changed city. She and the governor enjoyed a privileged position of power. Running one of the two major newspapers in Houston gave them entrée into the backrooms of city and state politics, where the real "work" and deals of the city were made.

Oveta wasted no time in picking up where she left off, rejoining her activities as a patron of the arts. She was on the board of directors of both the Houston Symphony and the Museum of Fine Arts at different times and supported both organizations throughout her life. She began collecting artwork for her own personal collection and soon filled her house and office with masterpieces bought on her behalf by Pierre Matisse, the son of the famous impressionist artist. Pierre, living in New York City, would send Oveta letters and pictures of pieces he thought she would enjoy, and buy them on her behalf, shipping the pieces she chose to her home in Houston.

One thing Oveta had become masterful at during her Army

career was delegating and getting help with her projects. She learned that one person can't do everything and was quick to enlist competent people to help her.

Just how did Oveta get all her work done? The *St. Louis Dispatch* gave a glimpse into her management style:

> Two secretaries at her *Post* office and a domestic staff of four at home help Mrs. Hobby with career and household duties. Day begins at 6 a.m. in the 22-room house bought and remodeled under her supervision in 1946. Household problems come first and by 8:15 a.m. Mrs. Hobby calls her office to have important mail read to her and give suggestions for the day.
>
> By 10:30 a.m. she is in her office [at the newspaper] ready for more mail and comments on the day's issue of the paper. Generally, the morning is spent with department heads. After lunch at home, she's back in her office at 2:30 p.m. for conferences with editorial department heads and for other meetings her civic responsibilities require. By 6:15 p.m. she is ready to leave her desk.
>
> "One thing about her experience in the Army," a secretary said, "she leaves her desk every night as clean as if a vacuum cleaner had been over it."
>
> And how does she get it all done?
>
> "I do one thing at a time, trying to put first things first," was her simple answer.[1]

With the end of World War II and the threat of Nazism under control, a new threat appeared on the horizon, the threat of communism.

Soon, accusations echoed over the radio waves and newspapers about the "Reds" taking over the country. Reds was the term used in reference to communists. The communists were lumped into the same category as liberals, progressives, Democrats, and left-wingers. Once a person was labeled as a communist, his or her job and livelihood were threatened. No reasonable person at the time considered people who were Democrats or liberals to be communists, but once a person was labeled as a communist, things could go wrong for him or her very quickly.

A group of powerful conservative women in Houston, known as the Minute Women, took as their mission the identification of communists. They used their considerable power to discredit those people they identified, rightly or wrongly, as communist.

During the same time, in the early 1950s, a Wisconsin senator by the name of Joe McCarthy climbed on the bandwagon and began a national campaign to eradicate communists from the United States. Hollywood celebrities were targeted and many lost their jobs, including the actor/comedian Charlie Chaplin, who was forced to emigrate to England to escape persecution.

It did not matter if a person actually *was* a communist, just the implication that they *might* be a communist was enough to damage their reputation, often forever.

This issue put Oveta in a tough position, both personally and in her capacity as head of the *Houston Post* with her husband. Governor Hobby, by this time in his mid-seventies, was more provincial and conservative than his wife, who was a dedicated Eisenhower Republican and internationalist. These differences in their political bents were played out on the pages of their newspaper. The governor's views were written in the paper's editorial columns by an old friend of his, Ed Kilman; Oveta's more liberal viewpoint was articulated by staff writers such as Marguerite Johnston and George Fuermann in the newspaper's articles.[2]

Speaking before the Alabama Press Association in February 1950, Oveta said, "When sensational charges are made . . . by vacant-minded or hysterical people . . . the charges are broadcast from coast to coast; and the public instinct is to accept charges as proof." She asked her journalist colleagues to emphatically ask, "What is your proof?" when these allegations arose.[3]

Oveta found herself somewhat between a rock and a hard place. On the one hand, she was against the anti-communist rhetoric being flung by her very own newspaper in Ed Kilman's editorial columns. On the other hand, Kilman was representing her husband's viewpoints.

Oveta tried to get Kilman moved to another job in the newspaper, but the governor refused to let her do so, protecting his right-wing colleague. When one of the more liberal reporters complained to Oveta about Kilman, Oveta showed her frustration by shrugging her shoulders, saying, "There comes a time in every marriage when a wife knows she has said all she can say about a particular matter."[4]

During this time, General Dwight D. Eisenhower, or "Ike," as he was affectionately known, won the Republican nomination for president of the United States. Oveta and Ike had a mutual admiration for each other. She had worked with the general both in Africa and England during World War II, and she got to know him well. During his presidential campaign, she became one of his biggest supporters and "used her newspaper resources for great effect" to help bolster his nomination.[5] She joined the group Democrats for Eisenhower and even went so far as to work in New York City as a leader of the national Citizens for Eisenhower organization during his presidential campaign. Her husband stayed in Houston to run the *Post* and support Eisenhower in that way.

Oveta spent most of her life in government and politics, in one way or another. "I think there's always a great respect between people when each is sure that the other is dedicated to the public welfare," she said. "If people are really interested in research and legislation, I didn't find that it made any difference whether they were Republicans or Democrats . . . Among men and women who are really dedicated to the best interests of this country, you've seen it many times, the crossing over of party lines."[6]

Oveta described Eisenhower as having amazing organizing skill "in welding together all the generals of the different commands and the different armies. It was a skill [she] never saw equaled."[7]

So when Eisenhower won the presidential election in 1952, he appointed Oveta the head of the Federal Security Administration, or the FSA, which implemented the Social Security Act, among other things. He appointed her with the understanding that the FSA would soon be promoted to a cabinet-level government department, and she would become part of his cabinet.[8]

Eisenhower chose Oveta Hobby to run the new department partly because Oveta was a Texan and he owed an election debt to Texas, and partly because she was a woman and he had promised to install women in positions of responsibility. But he chose her principally because she possessed a rare talent for tactful administration.

The Senate agreed with the president. Senate Minority Leader Lyndon Baines Johnson, a Texan himself, took Oveta under his wing and introduced her around Capitol Hill.

During her Senate confirmation hearing, Johnson said, "Texans are not always in agreement on everything. But there's one thing there's no disagreement on—that's Oveta. She's the type of woman you'd like to have for a daughter or a sister, a wife or a mother, or the trustee of your estate."[9]

Oveta took with her to the Senate Finance Committee hearing a seating chart that she had asked her son, Bill Hobby, Jr., to prepare. She wanted to be able to address each committee member by name.[10] When her name came up for the vote, the senators confirmed her in seven minutes. And just like that, she found herself head of an agency overseeing 36,800 employees and disbursing $4 billion a year. She was in charge of the Social Security Administration, the Public Health Service, the Offices of Education and Vocational Rehabilitation, and the Food and Drug Administration. In April 1953, all those departments were rolled into one big agency known as the Department of Health, Education, and Welfare (HEW). Oveta's title as Secretary of HEW made her the second woman in the U.S. to hold a cabinet-level position of power in American government.

When Oveta was sworn in, her husband, the governor, was asked if he thought his wife was the smartest person in Eisenhower's cabinet. Governor Hobby said, "'Course she is. And if she weren't, she'd have them thinking she was."[11]

An article in the magazine *Business Week* said of Oveta: "Observers can make two mistakes about Mrs. Hobby, either of them fatal. They can figure that, as a woman, she doesn't really know much about business. Or they can get the idea, for the same reason, that she can be pushed around."[12]

Said a 1953 *Time* magazine article called "Lady in Command,"

She looked small and feminine behind her broad mahogany desk, but she moved with the poise and confidence of a successful business executive, as she checked "yes" and "no" on a long list of requests for appointments and telephone priorities. Now and then she paused reflectively and puffed on a Parliament [cigarette], then turned back to work. Outside, down through the mazes, corridors and channels of

Health, Education and Welfare, the news was spreading that Oveta Hobby was a lady in complete command.

Oveta's life moved with the precision of a metronome. At home in Houston, she issues household instructions to her domestic staff at weekly meetings. A fitful sleeper, she keeps a notebook on her bedside table, makes frequent midnight notes on her "planned life." Her office appointments are lined up on a conveyor-belt schedule. Her double-handled calfskin bag, which she carries everywhere, is a special efficiency container which she designed for her business papers, her purse, and a Book of Common Prayer.[13]

Even after moving back to Washington, D.C., to head up the HEW, Oveta kept her hand in the matter of the Houston Red Scare from afar. The Minute Women insisted that Oveta had communist sympathies and charged that HEW was "socialistic."[14] At that point, Oveta had had enough. She used her behind-the-scenes power and proved herself a superb tactician. Oveta convinced the governor to stop Kilman's editorial Red-baiting, and the *Post* editorials became more moderate. The death blow to the Houston part of the movement came when Oveta gave the okay to publish an exposé of Houston's Red Scare groups, including the Minute Women. She ran the exposé on the front page of the *Post*, where everyone would be sure to see it, as part of a series by Ralph O'Leary.

The series of articles ran for ten days in October 1953. The articles were so well written, researched, and crafted that progressive groups around the nation started ordering reprints. The demand was so great that the *Post* printed a special edition containing only the exposé articles; twenty thousand copies sold. This action effectively began the process of discrediting the Minute Women and ending their vicious attacks on Oveta and the HEW.[15]

Oveta Culp Hobby, President Dwight D. Eisenhower, and Governor William P. Hobby examining the certificate appointing Oveta as the secretary of the Department of Health, Education, and Welfare. April 11, 1953. *Courtesy Getty Images.*

CHAPTER EIGHT

Mrs. Secretary and the Polio Epidemic

Never complain. Never explain.

OVETA CULP HOBBY

One of Oveta's first acts as Secretary of the Health, Education, and Welfare Department (HEW) was to devise a commission to study the areas of food and drugs. The government had an enormous responsibility to maintain the safety of these items, but Oveta didn't have the staff to accomplish what the law required her to oversee. After the commission made its report, she was able to get increased funds for the food and drug agencies and also increase the number of scientists working in these areas.[1]

But the biggest challenge Oveta and the whole country faced in the early 1950s was the polio epidemic. Poliomyelitis, or polio, for short, was a debilitating disease, leaving some sufferers permanently paralyzed or dead. One of the disease's tragedies was that many sufferers were children and young adults. These patients were often doomed to live their lives inside "iron lungs," mechanical devices that "breathed" for a person whose diaphragm muscles, which are used to control respiration, were frozen by the disease.

President Eisenhower's cabinet—notice that Oveta Culp Hobby is the only woman present. *Courtesy Corbis Images.*

The race for a vaccine to prevent polio was on between two prominent research scientists, Jonas Salk and Albert Sabin. Salk and Sabin differed in their methods for perfecting a vaccine. Salk took a tiny bit of the live polio virus and put it through a process which essentially killed the virus. He thought that injecting this "dead" virus into the human body would cause the body to produce its own antibodies, which would, in turn, fight and kill the virus. Antibodies are small "fighter" cells the body makes in response to an infection. These cells then find the "enemy," in this case the polio virus, and destroy the virus cells. Destroying the cells would prevent a person from contracting the disease.

Sabin's oral vaccine, on the other hand, worked in the intestinal tract to block the reproduction of the virus cells and prevent the virus from spreading throughout the body. But it would take Sabin seven more years to perfect his vaccine—it wouldn't be until 1962 that the Sabin vaccine was considered effective.

Salk conducted the largest clinical trial in history to date, and it showed that his vaccine was both safe and effective in treating the disease. Good timing, because summer—also known as polio season—was on its way. And by all indications, 1955 was going to be a year of severe and widespread infection. All steps were taken to produce as much vaccine as possible, as quickly as possible.

Only one glitch. Because Salk's technique had just been developed, large-scale vaccine manufacturing plants were not yet available to produce the amounts of vaccine required to make it accessible by the most vulnerable parts of the population.

Oveta, or Mrs. Secretary, as she liked to be called, and her consultants decided to have not one, but five different drug

President Dwight D. Eisenhower giving Dr. Jonas Salk a commendation for developing the Salk polio vaccine, as Secretary Hobby watches. *Courtesy Corbis Images.*

manufacturers work on producing the vaccine. This was necessary so that the millions of doses required to immunize the population would be on hand by the time polio season arrived.

The vaccine was licensed several hours after Salk's clinical trials report. Millions of doses from five manufacturers licensed in the United States, Canada, and Denmark proved effective, with no hazardous effects. Yet difficulties remained.

Seven of seventeen lots made by one manufacturer, Cutter Biologicals, contained live, virulent viruses. The Cutter vaccine caused 204 cases of polio in people. Of those 204, 75 percent, or 153 of the recipients, were paralyzed, and eleven died.

The Cutter incident was a tragedy. What went wrong with their inactivation procedure was not clear, and the results that followed were dramatic. Dr. Leonard Scheele, surgeon general of the United States, withdrew the Cutter vaccine from the market. The two head directors of the National Institutes of Health (NIH) stepped down, and a separate agency to ensure appropriate manufacturing standards and controls for medical compounds was created within the NIH.

Despite the tragedy of 1955, the effectiveness of the Salk vaccine was evident. In the time period 1946 to 1955, before the vaccine was distributed, the number of cases of poliomyelitis per year in the United States was 32,890, with 1,742 deaths. By contrast, after administration of the Salk vaccine, and before institution of the Sabin vaccine, the number of cases per year dropped to 5,749, with 268 deaths, despite the fact that universal coverage for all susceptible individuals had not yet been achieved. In Sweden, where only the inactivated vaccine was and is used up to the present, poliomyelitis was eliminated.[2]

In speaking about the polio vaccine in an interview, Oveta later said:

What we did was set up a regional system of distribution to be sure that what vaccine we had available was apportioned fairly, giving preference to the southeastern states where the incidence of polio is always higher. Then we made funds available really in the public health and public welfare for people who could not afford it. We originated the vaccine distribution program.

There were many congressional hearings on the Salk vaccine because it was a very controversial thing, as you know. And the questions would come whether it should come through public health or children's department or through public welfare, and finally we worked it out by regions and by states and got the fastest distribution. There were many problems in that vaccine because it looked as if it were going to be a terrible polio year. Our concern was to get this vaccine out as quickly as we could. So by going by the state and regions, we could actually get this vaccine out fast. If you'd gone some cumbersome method, it might have been sitting up there six months later after the polio season was gone.[3]

Oveta was clearly shaken by the Cutter Biologicals vaccination incident. Calls for her resignation as secretary of HEW hit the newspapers, containing claims that she was more interested in drug manufacturers' profits than in the health and safety of America's children. Nothing could have been further from the truth; Oveta felt terrible that this tragedy had occurred on her watch.

Many politicians were vocal in their criticism of the whole vaccination process and the way Oveta and her colleagues had handled the affair. Others came to her defense. Senator Barry Goldwater wrote her on June 6, 1955:

When one leaves the sordid atmosphere of Washington and gets out into the country, where American people live and think in a free way, one finds an entirely different attitude than [what] prevails here. I mention this to you, because every place I go over the United States I find nothing but high regard and appreciation for the work that you have done in developing the Department of Health, Education and Welfare.

I just want to add my thanks to those I hear expressed over the United States for the time that you have devoted, for the interest you have shown, and for the superb manner in which you have conducted your office. I hope, also, that the current rumors that you might retire to the more peaceful and more delightful atmosphere of Texas are not true, because we need you to carry on this work.[4]

Oveta's close friend, Marguerite Johnston, described the incident this way:

The Salk vaccine controversy apparently waved hotter in Washington and New York than in cities most heavily plagued by polio . . . and Oveta was caught in the crossfire of Democratic leaders against Republican administration. Houston had had summer after summer of polio epidemics, and Mrs. Hobby's children were here. The problem the vaccine posed was this: Should it be held back until all children could be inoculated simultaneously, or let out to protect as many as possible as soon as possible?

Here in Houston, where the hospitals filled annually all summer long with polio patients . . . there was no panic and no scramble. Parents wait decently for their children's name to come up on the lists held by private pediatricians and public health clinics. I know because I had four young children at the time, and was covering medicine and the Texas Medical Center for the *Post*, so I can guarantee my facts from two points of view.

Marguerite Johnston continues:

From this background, Mrs. Hobby was in no way prepared for 65-year-old women hammering on doctors' doors in New York, demanding vaccination for themselves.

There was no connection between her resignation and the Salk controversy. Governor Hobby had grown increasingly ill, and she had nominated her successor as early as February of that year. Governor then took a dangerous turn for the worse, and at that point, nothing was important to her but being with him.[5]

Joan Braden, Oveta's personal assistant at the HEW, told the story this way:

Oveta never let her strength show. It was, rather, revealed. She never raised her voice, never demonstrated anger, never said, "We'll get back at him" or "I'll take care of her." When she got word that her husband, Will, was dying in a Houston hospital, she put her coat on and was pausing to say goodbye to me at the office door when the Surgeon General of the United States rushed up, literally wringing his hands. "Mrs. Hobby, I think you ought to know that the Salk polio vaccine was released two days ago and I've just had reports that several children have died after taking it."

Oveta made a half turn toward her desk, dropped her coat on her chair, and looked full in Dr. Scheele's anguished face. She said quietly, "Dr. Scheele, we have met regularly at least thirty times since I took office, and thirty times I have asked you to report to me on the activities under your supervision. This is the first time you have mentioned that you intended to release the polio vaccine."

That was all. Oveta's husband was dying. She had to go. But as far as I know—and I think I do—she never mentioned to anyone, certainly not to the newspapers that Scheele had made a tragic mistake.

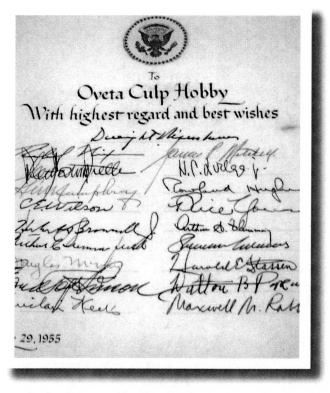

Document showing signatures of President Eisenhower's cabinet members. *Courtesy of the Oveta Culp Hobby Memorial Library, Central Texas College, Killeen, Texas.*

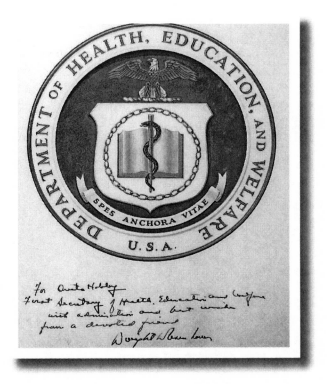

Commendation given to Oveta Culp Hobby for her service as secretary of the Department of Health, Education, and Welfare. *Courtesy of the Hobby family.*

Joan Braden continues:

Oveta took the blame, and the blame was headline news for days. And she took the cartoons that portrayed her as someone who was making up her face while babies died, as someone who had fumbled her job while she was fumbling in her purse for her lipstick, as someone who was, well, you know, a woman.

Imperturbably, she took it. Imperturbably, she sat on top

UNIVERSITY OF PITTSBURGH

SCHOOL OF MEDICINE

DEPARTMENT OF BACTERIOLOGY

VIRUS RESEARCH LABORATORY
THE MUNICIPAL HOSPITAL
PITTSBURGH 13, PENNSYLVANIA

24 February 1956

Dear Mrs. Hobby:

I had occasion to write, just the other day, the thought--
events, mellowed by time, make history. I suppose I could
say also--events unseasoned with time are often mistaken and
misunderstood.

Many times I had my hand on the telephone to call you; but, I
hoped that my silence told you there was little that I could
say.

I hope our paths will cross someday and the thoughts I wanted
to convey on these many occasions, when I felt the time was not
proper, may be expressed. That you had all my sympathy and
understanding is all that I want to say now.

I hope that your present activities are as rewarding as all
of the many great things you have done in the past.

Sincerely,

Jonas E. Salk, M. D.

Mrs. Oveta Culp Hobby
Houston
Texas

Dr. Jonas Salk's letter to Oveta Culp Hobby. 1956. *Courtesy
Woodson Research Center, Fondren Library, Rice University.*

Dear Dr. Salk:

Those were trying times - eased only by the present successful progress of the immunization program your vaccine made possible. Parents everywhere bless you in their prayers.

It was thoughtful of you to write me. Thank you for your note.

Best wishes always,

Sincerely,

Dr. Jonas E. Salk
Virus Research Laboratory
Municipal Hospital
Pittsburgh 13, Pennsylvania

February 29, 1956

Oveta Culp Hobby's reply to Dr. Jonas Salk's letter. 1956. *Courtesy Woodson Research Center, Fondren Library, Rice University.*

of this vast bureaucracy, over some of which she had no line of authority, the surgeon general, for example, was a presidential appointee. She stuck to her maxim with a will of iron: "Never complain, never explain."[6]

As soon as Oveta learned that her husband was ill, she called President Eisenhower and turned in her resignation. When George M. Humphrey, the Treasury Secretary, heard the news, he exclaimed, "What? The best man in the Cabinet?"

Despite pleas for her to stay on in her post, she was steadfast. "Nothing is as important as the governor," she declared, and

Oveta Culp Hobby as the only female member of the Eisenhower Exchange Fellowships, Inc. November 17, 1953. *Courtesy of the Oveta Culp Hobby Memorial Library, Central Texas College, Killeen, Texas.*

headed back to Houston to her husband, her family, and her newspaper.[7]

Oveta reported, "We had to stop the manufacture of the Salk vaccine, take it off the market for a while, put it back on the shelf because 14 children died from it, had some allergy to it . . . That to me was the most heartbreaking thing of all."[8]

Oveta was sorely missed in Washington. Her replacement, Secretary Folsom, at his first cabinet meeting, said, "Everybody is going to be awfully disappointed whenever they look down to this end of the table again." Later in the same meeting, a heated discussion took place in which several expletives were uttered. At the end of the meeting, President Eisenhower said, "If this is the kind of cabinet meeting we are going to have without Oveta, I am going to get her right back here."[9]

When she was in Washington, Mrs. Hobby was called "the most important woman in the country" in a newspaper feature. Asked for a comment about the story, Governor Hobby replied, "Well, I've known that for many years, and I knew some day the rest of the country would find it out."[10]

The timing of her resignation and her husband's quick return to health upon her arrival back in Houston suggest that she took a large part of the blame on herself, although Oveta never publicly admitted that her resignation had been due to the failure of the Cutter vaccine and resultant deaths and illnesses.

In her defense, she had been following the recommendations of the doctors and scientists in her employ as to the safety of the vaccine. Perhaps she naively trusted their interpretations of the data. But the vaccine was released without her knowledge, and she was unprepared for the crisis that followed. Because the vaccine-manufacturing technique itself was in the process of being developed, the quality control and fail-safe methods used on present-day vaccines were not yet in place.

Some of Oveta Culp Hobby's Accomplishments as Secretary of HEW

- Congress authorized $182 million to expand the federal-state-local hospital building program.

- Congress authorized $150 million to build more chronic disease hospitals, nursing homes, diagnostic and treatment centers, and medical rehabilitation.

- Organized the first White House Conference on Education.

- Proposed a three-year emergency plan to build $7 billion worth of schools.

- Oversaw the release and distribution of the Salk vaccine to prevent polio.

- Ten million people added Social Security coverage during her last year in office.

★　★　★

Murry Snyder, Assistant Press Secretary to President Eisenhower, July 13, 1955 The White House

Remarks by the President and Mrs. Oveta Culp Hobby in the Conference Room after the President accepted the resignation of Mrs. Hobby as Secretary of Health, Education, and Welfare.

THE PRESIDENT:

Well, Oveta, this is a sad day for the Administration. My mind goes back to the day I first met you in London—in

1942 I suppose it was when you came over there as head of the WAC Corps—something entirely new in my experience. But you were the first one that sold it to me, and I must say it proved itself, under your leadership, to be one of the finest organizations that the Army has ever had.

In these last two years—two years and a half—your talents have again been devoted to the service of your country, and most effectively. And I would think I could express the feeling of the Cabinet toward you by quoting the Secretary of the Treasury—I'm sure he wouldn't mind. The other day in my office, shortly after you had told me that you would have to go, I said to him that we were going to lose you. And his eyes popped open and he said, "What? The best man in the Cabinet?"

That is the feeling that the whole Cabinet has towards you. I assure you that none of us will forget your wise counsel, your calm confidence in the face of every kind of difficulty, your concern for people everywhere, the warm heart you brought to your job as well as your talents. We are just distressed to lose you, but the best wishes of the entire Executive Department—indeed, I think of the Congress and all Washington that knows you, will go with you as you go back, and we will be very hopeful that you will have many fine, happy years there from here on.

MRS. HOBBY'S REPLY:

Thank you very much, Mr. President. Mr. President, during the past 31 months, I have had the most singular opportunity. I have had an opportunity to serve with you, to serve a man whose entire life has been devoted to the people of the United States. I have had the most unfailing support and leadership from you in trying to develop sound programs for the American people in the field of health, education, and welfare. And as I look back over the 31 months, Mr. President, when you came to this Office, and realize what has transpired in those 31 months, I am a very, very happy citizen.

In those 31 months we have moved away from the shadow of war; we have moved into the greatest prosperity this country has ever known, with more people working, greater wages, and being able to buy more of the good things of life.

And now perhaps we stand in the area of widest peace, and perhaps on the threshold of a universal peace. When I think of what has been accomplished in your thirty-one months, I feel humble and grateful to have had a part in it. When I think of the people of the United States who have had their pensions and their social security protected by a stable dollar, Mr. President—the smallest variation in the purchasing power of the dollar in 42 years—the time we have kept records; when I think of the millions of people that have been given an opportunity under social security and the hundreds of thousands that will be given an opportunity under vocational rehabilitation, and when I think of the millions of people that will benefit from your wise policies in education—in letting the people of this country think through their own education problems and bringing them up here—I feel particularly blessed.

Now, Mr. President, as you go to Geneva for all of us, I believe that everyone of us will be praying that there, in that meeting, the first step will be taken toward a truly universal peace. And I for one, Mr. President, have never had such a privilege. I know this country would have been blessed at any time to have had your leadership, but in these critical years in world affairs, I truly feel that God had His hand on the United States in the kind of leadership you have given us.

THE PRESIDENT:

Oveta, if I had known that you felt like that, I never would have accepted your letter of resignation. Mrs. Secretary, I can still say that, thank you very much.

MRS. HOBBY:

Thank you, sir.

Oveta Culp Hobby, publisher, *Houston Post.* Used by permission, © Joe Baraban.
Courtesy of the Dolph Briscoe Center for American History.

CHAPTER NINE

Retirement and Philanthropy

It annoys me a little that people pull back and say,
"Well, a woman did that." Why not a woman?

OVETA CULP HOBBY

After retiring from her position as the secretary of the
Department of Health, Education, and Welfare in 1955, Oveta
took over the reins of the *Houston Post* with a renewed vigor
while tending to the governor. Shortly after her return to Houston, his health improved. For the next nine years, they worked
in "a single large room in their house or in adjacent offices at
the *Post*."[1] But Oveta remained active in the community and in
championing causes dear to her heart.

High on her list was civil rights. Both she and the governor
had been unwavering supporters of civil rights for all Americans, both personally and professionally. In addition to her
early involvement with the League of Women Voters, she had
a strong history of supporting black women as director of the
Women's Army Corps.

When the Supreme Court was due to hand down the *Brown
v. Board of Education* decision that desegregated the nation's
public schools in 1954, the *Houston Post* was ready. Page one

carried statements by every major religious leader in support of the decision.[2]

Oveta and Governor Hobby had a history of helping out people who would later become famous and influential. Kay Bailey was one such person. Kay Bailey graduated from the University of Texas Law School in 1967, one of thirteen women in a class of 390 graduates. At the time, no major law firms would hire a woman as a partner; indeed, as a woman Kay had a difficult time finding a job at any law firm in Houston. Discouraged, she decided to pursue a different way of using her law degree. Without an appointment, she dropped in to KPRC-TV, the Houston NBC television station owned by the *Houston Post*, which was owned, in turn, by Oveta and the governor.

Unfortunately, there was no job opening at the station, and

Walking to Governor William Pettus Hobby's funeral. Front row: Diana Hobby, Oveta Culp Hobby, Bill Hobby. Back row: Jessica Hobby Catto, Henry Catto. Children: Paul and Laura Hobby. *Courtesy Dolph Briscoe Center for American History.*

Kay Bailey had no journalism experience. Nevertheless, the local news director was intrigued because "no one with a law degree had ever applied for a job at KPRC before." He told the station manager they should find a place for Kay Bailey.

The station manager spoke to Mrs. Hobby, "who was enthusiastic about a young woman with a law degree working for the station. Oveta told the station manager that having her television station put the first woman on broadcast news was right up her alley."[3] And so, Kay Bailey was hired.

Kay Bailey Hutchison, now a former U.S. senator from the state of Texas, credits Oveta Hobby for giving her her first break in public life.

When Governor William Pettus Hobby died on June 7, 1964, at the age of eighty-six, LBJ was president of the United States. LBJ sent the following message to Oveta:

June 8, 1964

TEXAS and the nation are diminished by the loss of Governor Hobby. Throughout the last 30 years he was a wise, charitable, and loyal friend to me. He viewed the world with tolerant eyes and his wit and humor always salvaged a time of crisis and made it endurable.

As a Governor, as a publisher, as a counselor to the nation's leaders, as a husband, father, and friend, what he did in his lifetime and the honorable way in which he did it should serve as an inspiration to young men of our land. For the achievements of Governor Hobby are the works of good citizenship in its noblest form.

Lady Bird and I send you, Bill and Diana, Henry and Jessica, our love and our prayers in your time of grief.

LYNDON B. JOHNSON[4]

Three years later, on December 12, 1967, LBJ and Oveta together attended the ribbon-cutting ceremony when the Central Texas College and Library in Killeen were dedicated. President Johnson promised to give some of his papers to the library. The library was named the Oveta Culp Hobby Memorial Library in honor of Oveta's work for the Women's Army Corps.

Oveta was unable to attend the ceremony honoring her when her birthplace house in Killeen was designated with a historical marker, but she sent this message:

> My lifelong friends will know how greatly it disappoints me to not be in Killeen today for the dedication of this marker by the Killeen Sesquicentennial Committee.

Oveta Culp Hobby and President Lyndon Baines Johnson remained lifelong friends. Here she is attending a Christmas party at the White House. *Courtesy of the Oveta Culp Hobby Memorial Library, Central Texas College, Killeen, Texas.*

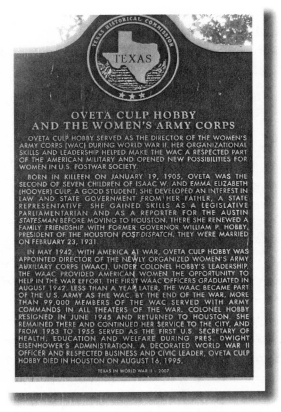

Historic marker outside Oveta Culp Hobby's birthplace in Killeen, Texas. *Courtesy Debra L. Winegarten.*

I love Killeen. In my childhood days, I knew every person in town, as did my parents and grandparents.

Killeen was a wonderful place in which to grow up. Our people were fiercely independent, but a caring people. They knew that with the joys of independence must come responsibilities. They assumed their responsibilities.

This was the Killeen that shaped the character, the ethical standards, the sense of responsibility and the independence of all who were fortunate enough to grow up there.

I wish I could be there now, at this moment, to feel again the home of my childhood. With all my heart, I thank you for this honor. No other could mean more to me than this honor from the community that gave me birth.[5]

Today, Killeen houses Fort Hood, home of the largest Army post in the U.S., with over 65,000 personnel. Oveta's name is prominently displayed at the post—both an elementary school and the fort's Soldier and Family Readiness Center proudly bear her name.

Texas stories were Oveta's specialty. She had been around men all her life, in the Texas legislature and at the *Houston Post*. Many of these men were or had been farmers or oil riggers, plainspoken men who swapped stories that would not have been told in Park Avenue apartments. Some of them were sidesplitting, but only if you had more than a glass of wine to go with them.

Joan Braden, Oveta's aide at the HEW, said of her, "Oveta was a tougher boss than any man for whom I've ever worked. She had grown up in a man's world, competing against men and competing successfully. By which I mean that often enough she had won. The effort had required more self-discipline than most women of her generation ever had to demand of themselves."[6]

Her granddaughter remembered that Oveta had to remind herself to make "small talk" with the wives when she went to parties. Because of her intellect and experience, Oveta was often more interested in the discussions the men were having. In 1978, a *Texas Monthly* article said, "Mrs. Hobby's skill at handling men was legendary. 'She just exuded this sort of sensuality. She could have her hand on your husband's arm and you wouldn't mind because you knew she wasn't interested in sex—just power.'"[7]

In 1983, Oveta sold the *Houston Post* to the Toronto Sun Publishing Company for about $130 million. Pat Roberson, an employee of the *Houston Post* for a number of years, went to the executive offices on the last day the Hobbys owned the *Post* to tell the staff goodbye:

> To my surprise, the offices were empty. I looked in the kitchen, and there was Mrs. Hobby, opening and closing the cabinet doors—not as if she was checking what was on the shelves, but more like she was taking a last look, as if she was thinking of all the years she'd been a part of the newspaper.
>
> "I hope I'm not intruding," I said to her.
>
> "Oh, no," she responded.
>
> "I wanted to tell you goodbye," I continued, "and to tell you how much I have enjoyed working for you and your family."
>
> She smiled and thanked me.
>
> "I promise you," I went on, "that we will take real good care of your newspaper."
>
> Mrs. Hobby smiled again. "Pat," she said, "I really would appreciate it if you would."[8]

With the newspaper sold, Oveta and her family company, H&C Communications, still owned five television stations.

Ron Stone, a television reporter for KPRC-TV, Channel 2, said:

> I remember when Mrs. Hobby was made a member of the Texas Business Hall of Fame. I went to report her *induction* on the 5 p.m. news on Channel 2, one of the television stations owned by the Hobbys. I looked into the camera and announced that Mrs. Hobby was *indicted*. Realizing my error immediately, I said, "I meant to say, 'Mrs. Hobby was *indicted*' a second time!"
>
> But what I meant to say was inducted.[9]

I walked into the Newsroom after the telecast, the phones were ringing off the wall, and everyone was laughing and saying, "Ron, that has to be Mrs. Hobby on the phone, and you are out of here!"

Indeed Mrs. Hobby was on the phone. She convulsed with laughter, and said, "You have just added credence to what all my friends say they think should have happened a long time ago!"

I tried to apologize, and Mrs. Hobby said, "Now don't worry about it," and then she began laughing again. Mrs. Hobby did not suffer fools lightly, but in this case, she let this fool get away with it.[10]

The end of another era came in 1992. At that time, H&C Communications, the Hobby family enterprise that owned their various media holdings, sold its five television stations. Among the purchasers, the *Washington Post* bought the Houston and San Antonio stations, while the Weather Channel bought the Nashville station.[11] The estimated selling price for all the stations was $600 million.[12]

With the selling of the newspaper and television stations, Oveta's hold on and work in broadcasting concluded. But her impact was not forgotten, and she was often called upon to comment upon current events, analyze, or give her perspective.

In her later years, Oveta had time to reflect on some of her earlier activities:

"It is true, I was the first woman to do several jobs that were once only open to men . . . It annoys me a little that people pull back and say, 'Well, a woman did that.' Why not a woman? I think we ought to get this out of the whole lexicon of thinking and writing, that surprise when a woman does something," she says, and pauses a moment before her hearty laugh erupts.

"You know, I was just thinking," she says, as her laughter ebbs, "men would come in my office, reporters, and they'd always look for that 'feminine touch' . . . and ask things like, 'Do you know how to make hollandaise sauce?' It just throws you off."[13]

The Associated Press's Biographical Sketch of Oveta, issued July 15, 1953, shows the extent to which the fact that she was a woman was apparently salient to the public. Oveta was compared to Miss Frances Perkins, the first woman to hold a cabinet position, that of secretary of labor under Franklin D. Roosevelt. The sketch noted that "Miss Perkins' hats were famous, while Mrs. Hobby was known particularly for her coolie hats. However, she liked all kinds of hats and had a large number. 'They really aren't frivolous,' she said, explaining: 'When you have to attend a lot of meetings in one day, a change of hat is the quickest way to freshen up.'"[14]

Oveta understood how hard it was for the media to view her as simply a competent *person*, regardless of the fact that she was also a woman. She told the following story, which shows that Oveta was not the only female to find herself in that position:

A friend of mine became president of Lord & Taylor, and I think she was the first woman head of a really big retail chain. I wired her and said, "Right On," or the equivalent that we said then, and she wrote me back and said, "You know, Oveta, during the war, I used to read the press on you and think, *she* ought to do better than that. Then at my first big press conference, a male reporter raised his hand and asked me what size shoe I wore. I finally realized, it's out of your control. They are going to get back to the woman thing."

Oveta added, "I'd like to live long enough to see people not be surprised by the fact that a woman succeeded in something."[15]

★ ★ ★

Oveta was a great collector of artwork and donated many of her prized pieces to the Museum of Fine Arts, Houston, for which she was a trustee for a number of years. An avid art collector starting after World War II, Oveta understood the importance of having great art available to the public.

Whenever Oveta got tired of a painting or wanted to make room for a new acquisition, she would donate several of her works to the Houston Museum of Fine Arts. Over the years, Pierre Matisse, a New York art buyer and the son of the famous painter Henri Matisse, acquired paintings from important artists like Joan Miró, Henri Matisse, and Modigliani for Oveta. During her period as secretary of HEW, Oveta had Pierre mail her paintings to Washington, D.C., so she could decorate her apartment there.

After the governor's death on June 7, 1964, and Oveta's retirement from the *Houston Post* and its subsequent sale, she moved to a large condominium apartment in the River Oaks area to be closer to her children and grandchildren. When she closed up the big house, she donated many of her large art pieces to the Museum of Fine Arts.

Fortune magazine ran a story in 1982 with its annual list of the nation's wealthiest people. Oveta's wealth was listed at $200 million, and her longtime friend, George Brown, $100 million. "Poor man," Oveta told Pat Bowman, her personal secretary, "I think I'd better call him today and see if wants to borrow some money!"[16]

In November 1984, she donated her collection of master drawings, valued at over $1,300,000, to the museum. Among the drawings were works from Degas, Gris, Matisse (four), Modigliani, and

Pablo Picasso (two). Oveta and the Hobby Foundation donated other types of artwork, such as a 1939 Marino Marini bronze sculpture, the *Pilgrim II*. Oveta also made outright cash donations to help the museum purchase pieces such as Picasso's *The Rower*.

✳   ✳   ✳

Oveta remained an avid reader throughout her life. Her granddaughter, Laura Beckworth, remembers that Oveta loved a good P. D. James mystery and always read the daily newspapers. Oveta enjoyed spending time with her grandchildren, often coming to their house when they got out of school so she could help supervise their homework. Laura thinks Oveta appreciated the chance to share in her grandchildren's lives—in part because during earlier years, she had been so busy with governmental responsibilities that she missed those moments in her own children's lives.

Oveta Culp Hobby, dubbed the "Sixth Most Well-Dressed Woman" in America. *National Dress Institute, New York.*

Laura remembers going over to the big house on Remington Lane before Oveta sold it. Her grandmother would let her dress up in her fabulous evening gowns and put on her jewelry. Laura remembers riding the elevator in the house down to the grand ballroom where she would pretend she was attending a great ball. She still misses not being able to call Oveta on the phone so they could discuss current events or the attendees at a Houston social event.[17]

Oveta died of a stroke on Wednesday, August 16, 1995, at her home in Houston, Texas. She was ninety years old.

Telegrams and letters poured into Houston from all over the country and the world. Lady Bird Johnson sent a telegram:

> Lyndon and I were so lucky to have shared your mother's life. She was one of the most able, brilliant and interest-ing people we had the good fortune to know. I recall many happy times of working together and enjoying Oveta's friendship. I hope you all will draw solace from her long and extraordinary life and great achievement.
>
> Lady Bird[18]

Mattie E. ("Patty") Treadwell, who served as an assistant to Oveta when she was WAC director, said:

> When Oveta Hobby died, I was told that her funeral instructions included the request that Mr. Jim Crowther and myself fold the flag and hand it to the family at the pri-vate graveside services. This flag was one that had hung in Governor Hobby's office and had covered his casket. It was heavy silk with gold fringe.
>
> I had never folded a flag in my life, so just before the funeral I practiced with a nephew who was a Scoutmaster.

At things turned out, the color guard from Fort Hood folded the flag and handed it to me, and I in turn presented it to the family.

I could not help but think that in a way Oveta Hobby's scheme was that the person who was there at the start of the history of her role in the Women's Army Corps should end it in this fashion.[19]

Oveta specified most of the details regarding her funeral. As in life, she wanted things to run as smoothly as possible and left instructions that the ceremony should be reviewed and rehearsed. She asked that her coffin be wooden and draped with the same flag that hung in Governor Hobby's office; afterwards, the flag was to be placed in the hands of her children, William and Jessica. She asked to be buried in the most presentable dressing gown she had left at the time. She also asked that Mrs. Bowman ensure that her hair was properly clean and tidy.

Oveta was a grand dame in the true sense of the word, living her life with dignity and ensuring that her final rites continued that tradition. This hard-working, tough-as-nails woman was quick to acknowledge the help of others in her life and to disparage her own contributions to her successes.

One hundred years after the birth of a small girl in a little town in Central Texas, the legacy of women in the military is due in large part to the leadership efforts of Oveta Culp Hobby.

Many of the careers women hold today are the result of Oveta's influence. Some of the social service agencies in the federal government today exist because of her tenacious vision. The tolerance, culture, and cosmopolitan nature of the city of Houston exist in part because one woman dared to follow her inner passions. May her story help you to discover and follow your own dreams and turn them into tangible realities.

Oveta Culp Hobby in her living room in Houston, Texas. *Courtesy Getty Images*.

CHAPTER TEN

Oveta's Legacy

In his book *The Power Elite*, C. Wright Mills describes sociology as "the intersection of history and biography."[1] Viewed from this perspective, Oveta herself is clearly a sociological phenomenon. She found herself the director of two major governmental entities during the middle of the twentieth century in America: the Women's Army Corps and the Department of Health, Education, and Welfare. Although she did not self-identify as a feminist, and indeed her son, Bill Hobby Jr., made it a point to say that she neither considered nor called herself a feminist, I think it is accurate to say that Oveta embodied and represented the feminist ideal: the equal treatment of both sexes in all areas of life, both personal and political.

Oveta is an unsung heroine of the women's movement. When she began her career as the director of the Women's Army Corps in 1942, the Army had identified fifty-four jobs that were considered appropriate for women to perform. By the time Oveta retired out of the Corps three years later, Army women were allowed to serve in 239 different job capacities—a 400 percent increase![2] When these former women soldiers returned to civilian life from their war duties, many were not content to only take on or return to the mantle of housewife. Because they were successful in their Army careers, they wanted to continue on in the workforce, either in the same or similar capacities, or in other jobs altogether. After participating in the war effort, whether as typists, telegraph operators, cooks, aircraft spotters, or in other roles, the women wanted to be able to continue working outside the home.

While serving as the secretary of the Health, Education, and Welfare Department, Oveta attempted to have Congress pass the National Health Reinsurance Program, which in essence would have been a national health care law that provided low-cost hospitalization insurance for many Americans who lacked insurance coverage. Before proposing the bill to Congress, she called the great insurance companies of the U.S., told them what she wanted to do, and asked for their guidance because she wanted to make sure the bill was drawn up correctly. The insurance companies sent her their best actuaries to help design the bill correctly from an actuarial viewpoint. This meant correctly calculating the expected life spans and illness probabilities for both men and women, and figuring out the health care costs associated with these statistics.

When it was time for the bill to come up for a vote, President Eisenhower invited these same insurance companies to send representatives to Washington to help answer congressional questions. Prior to the hearings on the bill, the president invited them over to the White House for lunch. During the course of lunch, Oveta explained the whole purpose of the program to them. After they left, they got together again and passed a resolution to support the bill. But Oveta was unable to get the American Medical Association to support the measure, and it was killed in Congress.[3]

On the question of whether or not she ever felt discriminated against in her jobs because she was a woman, she said, "You know, I never really found in any job I ever had anything to do with that it [being a woman] made any difference. If you're dealing with ideas and facts, it doesn't make any difference whether they come from a man or a woman. Now that isn't to say that some people may not have an emotional reaction. I know that's true. But I have never found this to be a handicap or a help. And I think you don't with reasonable people."[4]

Oveta may never have felt sex discrimination as a woman, but it was clear from reading media accounts that not only was her sex seen as an issue, but the press took many liberties in describing her. As was the custom of the time, newspapers often commented on what she was wearing, the way her hair was fixed or colored, and asked her questions related to how her husband felt about her working. We can say this is "differential treatment," because the press did not make the same types of comments about the men around her who were serving in similar capacities. From the media's perspective, she was viewed as something of an "oddity," or an "outlier," which added to her mystique.

Oveta also had certain personal rules pertaining to how she presented herself to the media. For instance, while serving both in the Women's Auxiliary Army Corps (later in the Women's Army Corps), she had a policy of making sure she was never smiling when she was photographed. She did not want people to think that she was having fun while serving in that responsible position.

She was a staunch supporter of equal rights, not only between men and women, but also among people of all colors. She insisted that African American troops in the Women's Army Corps were led by African American officers, and that the officers and troops received the same training as the Caucasian troops. When it was time to integrate the Houston schools and stop the practice of different schools for black and white students, Oveta made sure she was ready with editorials in her newspaper supporting these efforts. She gave Houston religious leaders a platform in the *Post* to express their support of integration. She understood the principles of "all people being created equal" described in the U.S. Constitution, and she did her best to ensure that the principle was carried out, in every area over which she had some influence.

At the end of the day, Oveta Culp Hobby personified the best qualities of being a human being—caring for herself, her family, her community, and her country. In the words of U.S. President John F. Kennedy, who came after she had performed much of her community service, "Ask not what your country can do for *you*, ask what *you* can do for your country." Our country asked much of Oveta Culp Hobby, and she met the challenge with the full force of her intellect, her vision, and her spirit. May her story serve as an inspiration to us all.

Time Line

★

MARCH 26, 1878 William Pettus Hobby born in Moscow, Polk County, Texas.

JANUARY 19, 1905 OCH (Oveta Culp Hobby) born in Killeen, Bell County, Texas, second of seven children of attorney Isaac William Culp and Emma Elizabeth Hoover Culp. OCH was named after a character in a romance novel.[1] "Her first name was an Indian word that her parents chose because it rhymed with Juanita, the name of one of her sisters."[2] "Her mother named her Oveta, an Indian word for 'forget,' after a character in a romantic novel and because the name rhymed with that of the Culp's first daughter, Juanita."[3]

1910 At age five, OCH refuses to sign a temperance pledge.[4]

1914 William Hobby Sr. elected lieutenant governor of Texas.

1915 Her father's favorite, OCH read the *Congressional Record* in his office at age ten.

1916 Hobby Sr. reelected lieutenant governor of Texas.

AUGUST 25, 1917	Hobby Sr. becomes acting governor of Texas.
SEPTEMBER 25, 1917	Hobby Sr. becomes governor of Texas when James Ferguson resigns.
1918	Hobby Sr. elected governor of Texas.
FEBRUARY 28, 1918	Texas legislature ratifies federal prohibition amendment.
MARCH 28, 1918	Texas women win the right to vote in state primary elections.
NOVEMBER 11, 1918	World War I ends. Culp family moves to Temple, Texas.[5]
1919	OCH goes with her father to Austin when he wins a seat in the Texas Legislature.[6] http://www.texasalmanac.com/history /timeline/20th/
FEBRUARY 5, 1919	Governor Hobby signs full suffrage bill.
NOVEMBER 1919	Texas voters pass prohibition amendment.
AUGUST 26, 1920	Nineteenth Amendment ratified by the last state needed for passage, Tennessee, giving the vote to women nationwide.
1917–1921	William P. Hobby Sr. serves as governor of Texas.
1922	OCH attends Mary Hardin-Baylor College for one year and studies liberal arts.[7]
UNKNOWN YEAR	OCH attends South Texas Law School and studies law (also has private tutors from 1921 to 1923).

1923 OCH works at the Capitol in Austin "codifying banking laws for the State Banking Commission, while letting her mother think she was taking a degree at the UT law school."[8]

1924 William Hobby, now a successful publisher and one of Texas's most popular governors, appointed president of the *Houston Post-Dispatch* newspaper.[9]

1925 A year shy of being old enough to vote, at age twenty, OCH appointed parliamentarian of the Texas legislature.[10]

1926–1930 "Attends classes at UT, audits lectures at its law school; becomes clerk for State Banking Commission and codifies the States of Texas's banking laws; clerks for the House judiciary and criminal jurisprudence committees."[11]

1926 OCH goes to work as a clerk in the circulation department of the *Houston Post-Dispatch*.[12]

1928 OCH serves as executive secretary of the Women's Democratic Club in Houston; helps plan Democratic National Convention held in Houston in 1928; works in Tom Connally's headquarters during his campaign for the U.S. Senate.[13] Works on senatorial and mayoral campaigns.[14]

1928 Between sessions as parliamentarian, OCH codifies state banking laws.

1929 Willie Cooper Hobby, first wife of former Governor William P. Hobby, dies. Oveta and William Hobby start dating outside of office hours.[15]

1930 OCH makes an unsuccessful run for the Texas House of Representatives, but is defeated by a member of the then-resurgent Ku Klux Klan.[16] "Her opponent whispered that she was 'a parliamentarian and a Unitarian.' She lost. It was the last time she ran for office."[17] OCH loses the race by four thousand votes.[18]

1930–1931 OCH is assistant to Houston city attorney: briefs law, writes opinions, drafts ordinances.

"Joins the *Houston Post-Dispatch* as assistant to a cartoonist, transfers to the circulation department, begins friendship with former Gov. William Pettus Hobby, her father's friend and now president of the newspaper and owner of KPRC Radio."[19]

1931 OCH returns to Austin as parliamentarian (serves through 1931, with incomplete terms in 1939 and 1941).[20] Elected state president of the League of Women Voters.[21]

FEBRUARY 23, 1931 OCH marries former Governor William Hobby Sr., then president of the *Houston Post*. She was twenty-six, he was fifty-three. They were married in Temple, Texas, by the Rev. C. R. Shirar. She goes to work for the *Post* as a research editor.[22] "William Hobby restores the newspaper's original name, the *Houston Post*."[23]

1931–1938 OCH is research editor, book editor, assistant editor at the *Houston Post*.

JANUARY 19, 1932 William P. Hobby Jr. is born, on his mother's twenty-seventh birthday.[24]

1932–1939 OCH is book editor and research editor of the *Post*, writes editorials and produces articles on community issues. Is the sole woman member on a citizens committee, which in 1935–1937 plans a flood control program for Houston. Writes *Mr. Chairman*, a handbook on parliamentary procedure which is adopted as a textbook by Texas public schools in 1938. Promoted to assistant editor of the *Post* in 1937. Appointed Texas chairman of the advisory committee on women's participation in the 1939 New York World's Fair.[25]

1936 OCH's book on parliamentary procedure, *Mr. Chairman*, is published by the Economy Company.

1936–1937 OCH is a member of the Texas Centennial celebration advisory committee.[26]

JUNE 12, 1936 Oveta and William Hobby survive airplane crash near Ferris, twenty miles south of Dallas. (*Washington Post* 6-13-36). They were flying home from Dallas where they had gone to hear President Roosevelt speak.[27]

1937 OCH's book on parliamentary procedure, *Mr. Chairman*, is reprinted by the Economy Company. She is elected a member of the American Society of Newspaper Editors—only the second woman in its membership.[28]

JANUARY 19, 1937 Jessica Hobby Catto born, on her mother's thirty-second birthday.[29]

NOVEMBER 1937 OCH appointed Texas chairman of the Advisory Committee on Women's Participation for the New York World's Fair, 1939.[30]

1938 OCH named executive vice president of the *Post*.[31] "Under her direction, the *Post* began covering events important to Houston's black community and featuring blacks in newspaper stories."[32]

OCTOBER 1938 *Mr. Chairman* adopted as a textbook in Texas public schools.[33]

1939 Hobbys buy the *Post* from Houston financier Jesse Jones, who also owns the rival *Houston Chronicle,* for about $4 million.[34]

JANUARY 1939 Serves as parliamentarian during the Texas legislative session.[35]

SEPTEMBER 1, 1939	Germany invades Poland, marking the beginning of World War II.
SEPTEMBER 3, 1939	France and Britain declare war on Germany.
SEPTEMBER 16, 1940	FDR signs the Selective Training and Service Act of 1940, passed by Congress two days earlier, starting the "first peace-time conscription in US history. . . . This Selective Service Act required that men between the ages of 21 and 30 register with local draft boards. Later, when the U.S. entered World War II, all men aged 18 to 45 were made liable for military service, and all men aged 18 to 65 were required to register."[36]
JANUARY 1941	Serves as parliamentarian during the Texas legislative session.[37] (Serves incomplete session.[38])
MAY 28, 1941	Congresswomen Edith Nourse Rogers introduces House Resolution 4906 (H.R. 4906), "a bill to establish a Women's Army Auxiliary Corps for Service with the Army of the United States."
SUMMER 1941	Public Music Association chartered in Houston, with OCH appointed as president; provides summer music concerts in Hermann Park.[39]

JUNE 1941 While in Washington, D.C., attending an FCC meeting on KPRC business, OCH receives a phone call from General David Surles asking her to come to the War Department and organize a section on women's activities; she refuses, but agrees to take home a sample of letters he's been getting from women nationwide and draw up organizational chart on ways women could serve.[40]

JULY 1941 "At the request of Gen. David Surles, she organizes in Washington, D.C., the new Women's Interest Section of the War Department Bureau of Public Relations, to furnish information to draftees' relatives. Nominated by Gen. George C. Marshall, Chief of Staff, she assists the group planning legislation for the Women's Auxiliary Corps; and is the only female representative of the War Department negotiating with the Bureau of the Budget and participating in Congressional hearings on the WAAC."[41]

DECEMBER 7, 1941 Japan bombs Pearl Harbor in Hawaii.

DECEMBER 8, 1941 FDR declares war on Japan after bombing of Pearl Harbor, U.S. officially enters World War II.

DECEMBER 11, 1941 Hitler declares war on the U.S. on behalf of Germany.

1942–1945 OCH is director of the Women's Auxiliary Corps and then the Women's Army Corps.

MAY 12, 1942	Bill signed creating the Women's Army Auxiliary Corps.[42]
MAY 16, 1942	Secretary of War Henry Stimson appoints OCH director and first commanding officer of the WAAC with the rank of colonel.[43] OCH takes oath of office, becomes the first woman to hold the rank of colonel in the U.S. military.[44]
SEPTEMBER 1942	OCH expands the listing of jobs women are certified to fill in the military from 54 to 239, expanding the corps from a few thousand women to 100,000.[45]
MID-OCTOBER 1942	OCH and Eleanor Roosevelt are invited by Queen Elizabeth to travel to England to "see how the British women are aiding in the war effort."[46]
OCTOBER 21, 1942	Eleanor Roosevelt, OCH, Betty Bandel, and others flew to England in one of the first commercial transatlantic flights to see how the British women were performing in the war effort.[47]
1943	WAACS receive full Army status and drop the word "Auxiliary" from the name, becoming the Women's Army Corps.[48]
MAY 16, 1943	OCH gives speech to the Texas State Society of Washington, D.C., recorded in the Appendix to the *Congressional Record* on May 17, 1943.
1943	"Awarded honorary LL.D. by Baylor University; Sam Houston State Teachers College; University of Chattanooga."[49]

MAY 16, 1943   OCH gives speech to the Texas State Society of Washington, D.C., recorded in the Appendix to the Congressional Record on May 17, 1943.

JULY 5, 1943   "Takes oath of office as Director, Women's Army Corps, becoming the first woman admitted to the new Army component."[50]

1945   "William P. Hobby and Oveta Culp Hobby establish the Houston-based Hobby Family Foundation, with philanthropic interests in health care, social services and community development."[51]

JANUARY 8, 1945   OCH is presented the Distinguished Service Medal by Secretary of War Henry L. Stimson.[52]

JULY 1945   OCH retires as colonel and leader of the Women's Army Corps, saying, "My mission . . . has been completed." She was exhausted.[53]

JULY 12, 1945   "Resigns as WAC Director, due to the serious illness of Will Hobby and the state of her own health. The 1941 vision of a corps of 25,000 women performing noncombatant service had broadened to recruit more than 99,000 by April, 1945, with WACS qualifying for 406 of the 628 military occupations."[54]

LATE 1945   OCH makes her first important purchases of art at the end of World War II.[55]

1946   "OCH made her classic quote, 'I think I'll like Houston if they ever get it finished.'"[56]

1948	Served as a member of the U.S. delegation to the U.N. Conference on Freedom of Information and the Press in Geneva.[57]
NOVEMBER 10, 1948	OCH named president of the Southern Newspaper Publishers Association.[58]
1950	OCH spends months working at national headquarters of Citizens for Eisenhower in New York.[59] Bard College awards her an honorary doctorate, Doctor of Humane Letters.
1952	U.S. experiences polio epidemic.
NOVEMBER 25, 1952	Eisenhower appoints OCH administrator of the Federal Security Agency, "the department of the federal government in charge of the health, education, and economic security of individual citizens."[60]
1953	The Federal Security Agency is renamed the Department of Health, Education, and Welfare (HEW) and its secretary made part of the president's cabinet.
APRIL 11, 1953	OCH appointed the nation's first secretary of Health, Education, and Welfare, a cabinet position; second woman to hold a cabinet position after Frances Perkins under FDR. OCH preferred to be called "Mrs. Secretary."[61]
JUNE 8, 1953	Ohio Wesleyan University awards OCH an honorary doctorate, Doctor of Laws.
DECEMBER 6, 1953	HEW Secretary Oveta Culp Hobby says U.S. schools lack 72,000 teachers and 345,000 classrooms.

NOVEMBER 1953	OCH serves as a trustee for the Eisenhower Exchange Fellowships, Inc., to train "rising young leaders" in non-Communist nations to help solve their countries' most urgent social and economic problems.
NOVEMBER 8, 1953	OCH appears on cover of the *Philadelphia Inquirer Magazine*.[62]
MARCH 22, 1954	OCH drafts "a new bill dealing with health insurance, to encourage private insurance companies to offer greater protection."[63]
1954	OCH praised as having the patience to postpone the announcement of the Salk vaccine until it had been properly tested.[64]
1955	OCH's resignation as Secretary of HEW "prompted Treasury Secretary George Humphrey to gasp, 'What? The best man in the Cabinet resigning?'"[65] Resigns to return to Houston and care for her ailing husband.[66] Takes position as president of the *Houston Post*.
MAY 1956	OCH awarded honorary Doctor of Human Letters from Mary Hardin-Baylor College.[67]
1960	OCH receives the Living History Award from the Research Institute of America.[68]
JUNE 7, 1964	William P. Hobby Sr. dies.
1966	OCH elected to the General Foods Corporation board of directors.[69]

1966–1975	OCH serves as a trustee for the Museum of Fine Arts, Houston.[70]
1967	OCH first woman named to serve on the board of trustees of Rice University.[71] OCH awarded the Carnegie Corporation Award for the Advancement and Diffusion of Knowledge.[72]
DECEMBER 12, 1967	Ribbon-cutting ceremony officially opening the Oveta Culp Hobby Memorial Library at Central Texas College in Killeen, with LBJ in attendance.[73]
1968	President Lyndon Johnson names OCH to the Public Broadcasting Board.[74]
JANUARY 20, 1969	Appointed an honorary Lifetime Member in the 147th Fighter Group, Texas National Guard, Ellington Field, Houston, Texas.
1978	Women's Army Corps disestablished.[75]
OCTOBER 18, 1978	"Presented with the George Catlett Marshall Medal for Public Service, the highest award given by the Association of the U.S. Army and awarded for 'selfless and outstanding service' to the nation. She was the nineteenth recipient of this award and the first woman."[76]
1979	Receives Rotary Club of Houston's Distinguished Citizen Award, in recognition of accomplishments to better the community.[77]
1983	OCH sells the *Post* to the Toronto Sun Publishing Co. for about $130 million.

APRIL 12, 1983	William P. Hobby Jr. swears in Ann Richards as governor of Texas.
APRIL 14, 1983	First U.S. Army Reserve Officer Training Corps established at a woman's university becomes the Oveta Culp Hobby Battalion at Texas Woman's University.
1984	Oveta inducted into the first Texas Women's Hall of Fame in the business and finance category.
JANUARY 19, 1986	Historical marker dedication and unveiling, Eighth Street and Young Avenue, OCH's home birthplace, Killeen, Texas.
1973–1991	William P. Hobby Jr. serves as Texas Lieutenant Governor.
1992	H&C Communications, Inc., a family enterprise, sells its five television stations, estimated selling price $600 million.[78]
1994	*Forbes* magazine lists OCH as the country's 287th wealthiest person, estimating the worth of her and her family's assets at $400 million.[79]
APRIL 16, 1994	Mary-Hardin Baylor College honors OCH at its homecoming.
APRIL 1995	OCH suffers stroke.
AUGUST 16, 1995	OCH dies at age ninety in Houston, Texas, of a stroke. Buried in Glenwood Cemetery, Houston, Texas.

DECEMBER 5, 1995   "Fort Hood dedicates the Oveta Culp Hobby University Center, offering bachelor's degrees in a program co-sponsored by Texas A&M University, Prairie View A&M, Tarleton State University, the University of Mary Hardin-Baylor, St. Mary's University in San Antonio, Central Texas College, and the University of Central Texas."[80]

OCTOBER 5, 1996   OCH inducted into the National Women's Hall of Fame in Seneca Falls, N.Y. The citation reads, in part, "You were respectful of the power you wielded in influential positions, you made the road smoother for the women who followed you."[81]

Notes

CHAPTER ONE

1. Al Shire, *Oveta Culp Hobby*, vi–vii.

2. Ibid., vii.

3. Evelyn M. Carrington, *Women in Early Texas*, xx.

4. Shire, *Oveta Culp Hobby*, v.

5. Ibid., 77.

6. Ibid., 55.

7. Patricia Lasher and Beverly Bentley, *Texas Women—Interviews and Images*, 74.

8. Shire, *Oveta Culp Hobby*, 11.

9. Ibid., 55.

10. Ibid., 10.

11. Women were granted the right to vote in the 1918 Texas primary elections.

12. Lasher and Bentley, *Texas Women*, 74.

13. "Hobby, William Pettus," *Handbook of Texas Online*.

14. Lasher and Bentley, *Texas Women*, 74.

15. Shire, *Oveta Culp Hobby*, 56.

CHAPTER TWO

1. David McComb interview, July 11, 1969.

2. Bill Hobby and Saralee Tiede, *How Things Really Work*, 14.

3. McComb interview.

4. Ibid.

CHAPTER THREE

1. Shire, *Oveta Culp Hobby*, 57.
2. Ibid.
3. Marguerite Johnston, *Houston: The Unknown City, 1836–1946*, 286.
4. Shire, *Oveta Culp Hobby*, 57.
5. McComb interview.
6. Mrs. T. H. Norman, "Lady of Killeen," 3.
7. Shire, *Oveta Culp Hobby*, 56.
8. Michelle Koidin, "Friends, Dignitaries Laud Oveta Culp Hobby," *Austin American-Statesman*, August 19, 1995.
9. http://www.lib.utexas.edu/taro/ricewrc/00038/rice-00038.html
10. McComb interview, 2.
11. Barron, "Oveta Culp Hobby."
12. James Anthony Clark and Weldon Hart, *The Tactful Texan*, 171.
13. http://www.lib.utexas.edu/taro/ricewrc/00038/rice-00038.html
14. McComb interview.
15. Barron, "Oveta Culp Hobby."
16. http://www.lib.utexas.edu/taro/ricewrc/00038/rice-00038.html
17. Ann Fears Crawford and Crystal Sasse Ragsdale, *Women in Texas*, 276.
18. Koidin, "Friends, Dignitaries."
19. McComb interview, 26.
20. Marguerite Johnson Barnes, "KPRC note."
21. McComb interview, 5.
22. Johnston, *Houston*, 336.

CHAPTER FOUR

1. Johnston, *Houston*, 337.
2. Shire, *Oveta Culp Hobby*, vi.
3. Ann Fears Crawford and Crystal Sasse Ragsdale, *Women in Texas*, 276.
4. Johnston, *Houston*, 337.
5. Shire, *Oveta Culp Hobby*, 11.

6. Johnston, *Houston*, 337.

7. Ibid.

8. http://www.tshaonline.org/handbook/online/articles/HH/fho 86.html

9. Mattie E. Treadwell, *United States Army in World War II Special Studies: The Women's Army Corps*, 28.

10. Ibid., 29.

11. Ibid.

12. Ibid.

13. Ibid., 30.

14. Ibid., 45.

CHAPTER FIVE

1. http://www.commandposts.com/2012/05/May-15-1942-formation-of-the-womens-auxiliary-army-corps/oveta-culp-hobby/

2. "WAAC: U.S. Women Troop to Enlist in Army's First All-Female Force," *Life*, June 8, 1942, 26.

3. Treadwell, *United States Army*, 50.

4. http://www.tshaonline.org/handbook/online/articles/fho86

5. http://www.tshaonline.org/handbook/online/articles/fho86

6. http://www.tshaonline.org/handbook/online/articles/fho86

7. Treadwell, *United States Army*, 6.

8. Treadwell, *United States Army*, 51.

9. http://www.tshaonline.org/handbook/online/articles/fho86

10. http://www.tshaonline.org/handbook/online/articles/fho86

11. http://www.tshaonline.org/handbook/online/articles/fho86

12. You can view the full address here: http://www.youtube.com/watch?v=XxML6I2JGbo.

13. Johnston, 1991:338.

14. Ron Tyler, Janice Pinney, and Colleen Kain, *Proceedings of the Annual Meeting at Corpus Christi*, 108.

15. Sylvia J. Bugbee, ed., *An Officer and a Lady*, 33–34.

16. Ibid.

17. Ibid., 40.

18. Eleanor Roosevelt, *This I Remember*, 262.

19. Bugbee, *Officer and a Lady*, 53.
20. Shire, *Oveta Culp Hobby*, 3.
21. http://www.tshaonline.org/handbook/online/articles/fho86

CHAPTER SIX

1. Treadwell, *United States Army*, 106.
2. Ibid., 119.
3. Ibid.
4. Johnston, *Houston*, 340.
5. Bugbee, *Officer and a Lady*, 129–130.
6. Ibid.
7. Elizabeth W. Fernea and Marilyn P. Duncan, eds., *Texas Women in Politics*, 21.
8. http://www.youtube.com/watch?v=a8QKsTKRYSO.
9. http://www.u-s-history.com/pages/h1682.html.
10. http://www.magiclink.com/web/lostheroines/webdoc5.htm.
11. Johnston, *Houston*, 339.
12. Bugbee, *Officer and a Lady*, 146.
13. Johnston, *Houston*, 340.
14. Ibid., 339–340.
15. Bugbee, *Officer and a Lady*, 183, 185.
16. Lasher and Bentley, *Texas Women*, 76.
17. Shire, *Oveta Culp Hobby*, 58.
18. Lasher and Bentley, *Texas Women*, 76.

CHAPTER SEVEN

1. Martha Cole, "First WAC Head Now Busy Publisher."
2. Don E. Carleton, *Red Scare: Right-Wing Hysteria, Fifties Fanaticism, and Their Legacy in Texas*, 84–85.
3. Ibid., 87.
4. Ibid., 86–87.
5. Ibid., 229.
6. McComb interview, 13–14.
7. Ibid., 7.

8. Carleton, *Red Scare*, 230.

9. "Lady in Command," *Time*, May 4, 1953.

10. Private email to author from Bill Hobby, Jr., February 17, 2013.

11. "Mrs. Hobby Now Wields Quieter Form of Clout," *Victoria Advocate*, May 15, 1988.

12. "Oveta Culp Hobby's New Job," *Business Week*, May 16, 1953.

13. "Lady in Command."

14. Carleton, *Red Scare*, 231.

15. Ibid., 245.

CHAPTER EIGHT

1. McComb interview, 18.

2. Michael A. Oldstone, *Viruses, Plagues, and History*, 108–109.

3. McComb interview, 21.

4. Letter from Barry Goldwater, June 6, 1955.

5. Marguerite Johnston, undated interview.

6. Joan Braden, *Just Enough Rope: An Intimate Memoir*, 60–61.

7. Barron, "Oveta Culp Hobby."

8. Judith Serrin, "Advice to Cabinet Women," 3C.

9. Letter to Oveta dated August 5, 1955 from the Assistant to the President, Washington, D.C. [Fondren archives].

10. Michael Shannon, "They Built Houston."

CHAPTER NINE

1. Barron, "Oveta Culp Hobby."

2. Tyler et al., *Proceedings*, 108.

3. Kay Bailey Hutchison, *American Heroines: The Spirited Women Who Shaped Our Country*, 251.

4. Lyndon B. Johnson, "Message to Mrs. Oveta Culp Hobby on the Death of Former Governor William P. Hobby of Texas."

5. *Killeen Daily Herald*, January 19, 1986.

6. Braden, *Just Enough Rope*, 66–67.

7. Hurt, "Last of the Great Ladies," 148.

8. Shire, *Oveta Culp Hobby*, 40.

9. "Indicted" means having formally charged or accused someone of a serious crime; "inducted" means having admitted someone to an organization.

10. Shire, *Oveta Culp Hobby*, 44.

11. Private email to author from Bill Hobby Jr., February 17, 2013.

12. Koidin, "Friends, Dignitaries."

13. Lasher and Bentley, *Texas Women*, 79.

14. Associated Press Biographical Sketch, "Mrs. Oveta Culp Hobby."

15. Lasher and Bentley, *Texas Women*, 79.

16. Shire, *Oveta Culp Hobby*, 9.

17. Laura Beckworth, in an interview with the author, 2009.

18. Telegram to William P. Hobby Jr., August 18, 1995.

19. Shire, *Oveta Culp Hobby*, 48.

CHAPTER TEN

1. C. Wright Mills, *The Power Elite: New Edition*, xx.

2. Lasher and Bentley, *Texas Women*, 76.

3. McComb interview, 20.

4. McComb interview, 11–12.

TIME LINE

1. Koidin, "Friends, Dignitaries."

2. Barron, "Oveta Culp Hobby."

3. Crawford and Ragsdale, *Women in Texas*.

4. Barron, "Oveta Culp Hobby."

5. Shire, *Oveta Culp Hobby*, 57.

6. Barron, "Oveta Culp Hobby."

7. Fernea and Duncan, eds., *Texas Women in Politics*, 20.

8. Ibid.

9. Ibid.

10. Barron, "Oveta Culp Hobby."

11. Shire, *Oveta Culp Hobby*, 57.

12. Fernea and Duncan, eds., *Texas Women in Politics*, 20.

13. Shire, *Oveta Culp Hobby*, 57.

14. Barron, "Oveta Culp Hobby"; Crawford and Ragsdale, *Women in Texas*, 274.

15. Fernea and Duncan, eds., *Texas Women in Politics*, 20.

16. Koidin, "Friends, Dignitaries."

17. Barron, "Oveta Culp Hobby"; Crawford and Ragsdale, *Women in Texas*, 274–275.

18. Shire, *Oveta Culp Hobby*, 57.

19. Ibid.

20. Ibid.

21. Johnston, *Houston*, 286.

22. Koidin, "Friends, Dignitaries."

23. Shire, *Oveta Culp Hobby*, 57.

24. Barron, "Oveta Culp Hobby."

25. Shire, *Oveta Culp Hobby*, 57.

26. Oveta Culp Hobby Papers, Woodson Research Center.

27. Johnston, *Houston*, 303–304.

28. Oveta Culp Hobby Papers, Woodson Research Center.

29. Barron, "Oveta Culp Hobby."

30. Oveta Culp Hobby Papers, Woodson Research Center.

31. Koidin, "Friends, Dignitaries."

32. Crawford and Ragsdale, *Women in Texas*, 276.

33. Oveta Culp Hobby Papers, Woodson Research Center.

34. Koidin, "Friends, Dignitaries."

35. Crawford and Ragsdale, *Women in Texas*, 274.

36. http://en.wikipedia.org/wiki/Selective_Training_and_Service_Act_of_1940.

37. Crawford and Ragsdale, *Women in Texas*, 274.

38. Shire, *Oveta Culp Hobby*, 57.

39. Johnston, *Houston*, 363.

40. Ibid., 336.

41. Shire, *Oveta Culp Hobby*, 57.

42. Crawford and Ragsdale, *Women in Texas*, 277.

43. Ibid.

44. Shire, *Oveta Culp Hobby*, 57.

45. Crawford and Ragsdale, *Women in Texas*, 277.

46. Bugbee, ed., *Officer and a Lady*, 40.

47. Roosevelt, *This I Remember*, 262.

48. Crawford and Ragsdale, *Women in Texas*, 277.

49. Shire, *Oveta Culp Hobby*, 57.

50. Ibid.

51. Messa, "Hobby Family Foundation."

52. Shire, *Oveta Culp Hobby*, 47.

53. Crawford and Ragsdale, *Women in Texas*, 277.

54. Shire, *Oveta Culp Hobby*, 58.

55. Ibid., 5.

56. Johnston, *Houston*, 393.

57. Shire, *Oveta Culp Hobby*, 16.

58. Crawford and Ragsdale, *Women in Texas*, 278.

59. Ibid., 279.

60. Ibid.

61. Ibid., 280.

62. Shire, *Oveta Culp Hobby*, 38.

63. Crawford and Ragsdale, *Women in Texas*, 280.

64. Koidin, "Friends, Dignitaries."

65. Crawford and Ragsdale, *Women in Texas*, 280–281.

66. Koidin, "Friends, Dignitaries."

67. Hobby and Catto, *Oveta Culp Hobby*, vi.

68. Fernea and Duncan, eds., *Texas Women in Politics*, 22.

69. Crawford and Ragsdale, *Women in Texas*, 281.

70. Shire, *Oveta Culp Hobby*, 6.

71. Crawford and Ragsdale, *Women in Texas*, 281.

72. Fernea and Duncan, eds., *Texas Women in Politics*, 22.

73. Shire, *Oveta Culp Hobby*, 31.

74. Crawford and Ragsdale, *Women in Texas*, 281.

75. Shire, *Oveta Culp Hobby*, 37.

76. Crawford and Ragsdale, *Women in Texas*, 281.

77. Shire, *Oveta Culp Hobby*, 41.

78. Koidin, "Friends, Dignitaries."

79. Ibid.

80. Shire, *Oveta Culp Hobby*, 60.

81. Ibid.

Glossary

acclaim To announce or proclaim with enthusiastic approval.

actuary A mathematician, usually working in the insurance industry, who computes the statistical probabilities for the chances of people developing certain diseases, as well as their life spans, among other things.

amendment As relates to a document, such as the Texas or U.S. constitution: a phrase or statement which adds to or clarifies certain provisions of a document.

antibodies Small cellular particles in a person's bloodstream that act as "fighter" cells to kill harmful viruses or bacteria in a person's body.

apportioned To divide or distribute according to some rule.

appropriation When a governmental body such as a legislature formally gives permission for a certain sum of money to be distributed for a specific purpose.

ATS (England) Auxiliary Territorial Services.

biennial An event occurring once every two years.

bill Proposed language submitted to a legislative body for consideration into becoming a state or national law.

blacklisting Placing a person's name on a roster of people who are accused of a certain—often suspicious, illegal, or unsavory— behavior, such as being a "communist."

black market Illegally buying or selling goods.

Brown v. Board of Education Desegregation law that declared "separate but equal" educational facilities for black and white students unconstitutional.

cabinet The U.S. president's advisory board, made of the directors of the federal government's executive departments.

capitalism An economic system in which individuals or corporations own the means of production.

Caucasian A racial classification term, used to designate "white" people.

cesarean section Delivering a baby by cutting the mother's abdomen open to retrieve the infant.

Chautauqua A traveling educational group, popular in the late nineteenth and early twentieth centuries, that provided performances in U.S. towns during the summer months.

civilian A nonmilitary person.

codify To arrange rules or laws into a system.

communism A type of social system in which property is owned by the community or the state.

community chest A fund for local welfare activities, made from voluntary contributions.

Congressional Record A daily transcript of the congressional sessions' discussions.

conscription Mandatory enrollment into military duty.

convalesce The process of recovering from an illness.

D-Day June 6, 1944, the day during World War II that the Allied Forces invaded Western Europe.

democracy A type of government run on the principles of equality and justice, where people exercise their rights and elect their government officials.

diaphragm A muscular wall separating the chest cavity from the stomach in mammals.

dishonorably discharged Being let go from military service for a serious offense of regulations.

dispensary A place where medicine is given out.

Distinguished Service Medal An award given for "exceptionally meritorious performance of a duty of great responsibility."

draft Mandatory enrollment into military duty.

elocution The study and practice of public speaking.

epidemic The rapid, often uncontrollable spread of a disease.

estate The possessions, both property and monetary, a person leaves to other people, after he or she dies.

expletives Another name for curse words.

Great Depression A period of low business activity beginning with a big stock market crash in October 1929 and continuing through most of the 1930s.

hollandaise sauce A culinary sauce made from lemons, egg yolks, butter, and seasonings.

illegitimate Refers to children who are born to a man and a woman who are not married to each other.

incubation The process of having a favorable environment in which to grow or hatch things, like bacteria or eggs.

indictment A serious charge of accusation, often stemming from someone violating a law.

induction Formally installing someone into an office.

inoculation A way of delivering medicine into a person's body by inserting a needle into a body part, often an arm or buttock, and injecting the medicine.

integration The practice of doing away with segregation—that is, of allowing people of different races to dwell together, go to school together, swim in the same pools together, eat at the same restaurants, use motels and hotels, drink from the same water fountains, and use the same bathrooms.

interred Jailed or imprisoned.

jurisprudence The philosophy of law.

khaki A yellowish-brown color, often referred to as the color of which military uniforms are made.

Ku Klux Klan A secret organization founded in the southern U.S. designed to intimidate blacks, Jews, and Catholics.

legislature An elected group of people whose job it is to make, enact, and change laws.

lexicon Another name for a dictionary.

Henri Matisse A famous French painter from the impressionism period of art.

Joe McCarthy era A time period during the 1950s when some progressive American citizens and military members were accused, often falsely, of being communists, and made to lose their jobs and reputations.

military-industrial complex A term attributed to President Dwight Eisenhower in his last speech, warning against a runaway partnership between the military and industrial capitalists.

Minute Women A group of Houston Republican women whose mission was to uncover communists during the McCarthy era.

Joan Miró A Spanish painter from the surrealist period of art.

Modigliani An Italian painter and sculptor.

NAACP National Association for the Advancement of Colored People.

Negro The name used, prior to the 1960s, to refer to people of African origin in the United States.

Nineteenth Amendment (to the U.S. Constitution) This constitutional amendment, adopted on August 26, 1920, guaranteed women the right to vote. The law reads, "The right of citizens of the United States to vote shall not be denied or abridged by the United States or by any state on account of sex." http://www.history.com/this-day-in-history/19th-amendment-adopted.

parliamentarian An expert in the rules and procedures that govern formal organizations such as clubs or legislative bodies.

phonograph A media player that uses large, round, flat plastic disks called records, on which music or speech was recorded.

physiotherapists Medical specialists trained to work with people who have problems with their muscles.

Picasso A Spanish painter instrumental in popularizing the abstract form of art.

polio The shortened form of the disease poliomyelitis.

poliomyelitis A disease caused by a virus, which could cause paralysis and/or death and often strikes young children.

power elite a sociological term referring to a class of people in a society who have access to money and resources and use that access to control things in society, often behind the scenes.

precedent An example that serves as a guide for a later situation.

primary A preliminary election where voters choose candidates to run for upcoming political offices.

Prohibition The practice of not allowing people to drink alcohol.

pyramids Stone buildings located in the town of Giza, outside Cairo, Egypt, built by Egyptian kings (pharaohs) beginning in 2584 BCE.

racism The practice of treating people differently based on the color of their skin or their place of birth.

Reds The nickname given to people who are or are assumed to be members of the Communist Party.

remuneration Payment for services rendered.

resolution A formal opinion expressed by or voted on by an organization, such as a legislature.

respiration Another name for the act of breathing.

Jonas Salk The medical doctor credited with creating the vaccine technique used to make the polio vaccine, which helped eradicate the polio epidemic.

segregation The practice of separating groups of people based solely on their race, i.e., sending black and white children to different schools or making black and white troops live in separate barracks from each other.

sesquicentennial The time frame of 150 years.

solvent Having enough money to pay one's debts.

special session A meeting of the Texas legislature, called at the request of the Texas governor, to deal with "emergency" issues not covered during the regular legislative session. A special session cannot last longer than thirty days, although a governor can call for a second special session if the business does not get completed during the first special session.

stenographer A person who transcribes spoken words or dictation and turns the words into a written document.

suffrage The ability of an individual or group of individuals to vote in elections; the right to vote.

tactician Someone who plans strategies.

telegraph An early communication method, predating the telephone, where messages could be transmitted over wires using a series of dots and dashes representing the letters of the alphabet.

temperance Refraining from drinking alcohol.

tenure The time period that one holds an office or position.

terra firma Literally "solid earth," but the phrase is used to mean "solid ground."

torpedo A weapon in the form of a missile fired from a battleship or submarine.

trustee A person given the power to perform legal duties on behalf of another person, often because someone has died or become physically or mentally unable to carry out those duties.

Unitarian A member of a religious denomination that stresses individual freedom of belief, the free use of reason in religion, a united world community, and liberal social action.

vaccine A potion, often delivered via an injection, designed to prevent the recipient from developing a disease.

virus A tiny microbe capable of producing a disease in a plant or animal.

WAAF (England) Women's Auxiliary Air Force.

war bonds A type of financial instrument sold by governments during times of war to help pay for the war.

Woman's Christian Temperance Union An organization founded "by women who were concerned about the destructive power of alcohol and the problems it was causing their families and society . . . The WCTU is now considered the oldest voluntary, nonsectarian women's organization in continuous existence in the world." (http://www2.potsdam.edu/hansondj/Controversies /Womans-Christian-Temperance-Union.html)

World War II A global conflict that lasted from 1939 to 1945.

Selected Websites and Resources

★

"1955 Polio Vaccine Trial Announcement." University of Michigan, School of Public Health, http://www.sph.umich.edu/about/polio announcement.html.

"Catto, Patron of Charities, Dies at 72." My San Antonio, October 1, 2009, Obituary of Jessica Hobby Catto, Oveta's daughter, http://www.mysanantonio.com/default/article/Catto-patron-of-charities-dies-at-72-842249.php.

"Eisenhower's Cabinet Meets." 1953. Budget Films Stock Footage. Short speech by Oveta Culp Hobby after the new cabinet department of Health, Education and Welfare was established, http://www.budgetfilms.com/clip/8124/.

"First U.S. Army Women Arrive in England. 1943." National Archives and Records Administration, ARC 38790, http://www.archive.org/details/gov.archives.arc.38970.

"First Woman Honored with Legion of Merit." A brief history of Colonel Westray Battle Boyce, who succeeded Oveta Culp Hobby as the second director of the Women's Army Corps when Oveta retired, http://www.waymarking.com/waymarks/WM810R_First _woman_honored_with_Legion_of_Merit_Rocky_Mount_NC.

Guide to the Oveta Culp Hobby Papers. Dwight D. Eisenhower Library, Abilene, Kansas, http://eisenhower.archives.gov/Research /Finding_Aids/pdf/Hobby_Oveta_Papers.pdf.

Guide to the Oveta Culp Hobby Papers, 1817–1995. Rice University, Houston, Texas, http://www.lib.utexas.edu/taro/ricewrc/00038 /rice-00038.html.

Ham Slice 17: TV in Houston. A brief history of the Hobbys starting

the first television station in Houston, Texas, http://www.youtube
.com/watch?v=5vWANZgErOw.

Hobby Family Bibliography, Bill Hobby Jr., http://www.billhobby
.com/pdf/HobbyFamilyBibliography.pdf.

"How a Bill Becomes a Law." http://www.house.state.tx.us/resources
/bill2law.htm.

Lyndon B. Johnson, "Message to Mrs. Oveta Culp Hobby on the
Death of Former Governor William P. Hobby of Texas," June 8,
1964. Online by Gerhard Peters and John T. Woolley, the American Presidency Project, http://www.presidency.ucsb.edu/ws/index
.php?pid=26301.

Medical Milestones-Polio. HealthCareNewsNtwrk, http://www.you
tube.com/watch?v=IPGW4f7GR6M.

NHD 2009: Jonas Salk: The Man Who Saved the Children, http://
www.youtube.com/watch?v=H6NkM61HlB8.

Oveta Culp Hobby. *Encyclopedia Britannica* article, http://images
.google.com/imgres?imgurl=http://media-2.web.britannica.com
/eb-media/08/21608-003-C3A92A99.gif&imgrefurl=http://www
.britannica.com/EBchecked/topic/268497/Oveta-Culp-Hobby
&usg=__pujBxlpFhjqkDquofSy_yLbDMSM=&h=140&w=100
&sz=6&hl=en&start=103&tbnid=2jcioh10Nl_SoM:&tbnh
=93&tbnw=66&prev=/images%3Fq%3Doveta%2Bculp%2Bhobby
%26ndsp%3D18%26hl%3Den%26sa%3DN%26start%3D90.

Oveta Culp Hobby. First Day of Issue Stamp. April 15, 2011. USA
Philatelic, http://www.beyondtheperf.com/stamp-releases/oveta
-culp-hobby.

"Oveta Culp Hobby: A Newspaperwoman Speaks." March 23, 1953.
Excerpts from Oveta's speech as the first woman speaker in the his-
tory of the Economic Club, http://www.econclubchi.org/History
/Excerpts_OvetaCulpHobby.pdf.

Oveta Culp Hobby. November 1943. "When Girls are Soldiers." Article for the Association for Supervision and Curriculum Development, http://www.ascd.org/ASCD/pdf/journals/ed_lead/el_19
4311_hobby.pdf.

"Pallas Athene Insignia and Award." Women's Army Corps Veter-
ans' Association. History and background of adoption of Pallas
Athene by the WAC, http://www.armywomen.org/award.shtml.

"Prenatal Memories of the Governor's Mansion, Bill Hobby to Mansion Docents, January 12, 2010," http://www.hobbycomm.com/wph/Essays/Mansion%20History.pdf.

Texas Legislative Reference Library, http://www.lrl.state.tx.us/gen Info/FAQ.cfm.

Texas Statesman William Pettus Hobby (1878–1964). The Historical Marker Database, http://www.hmdb.org/marker.asp?marker=35316.

The Texas Underground: A Guide to the Graves of Texans Past. Brief biography and picture of Oveta Culp Hobby's gravesite, http://the texasunderground.blogspot.com/2010/03/oveta-culp-hobby.html.

U.S. Army Women's Museum, http://www.history.army.mil/html/museums/showcase/women/awm_05.html.

"U.S. Rushes New Naval Bases in Pacific (1942)," U.S. National Archives. Vintage footage showing Oveta Culp Hobby in her new role as the director of the Women's Army Auxiliary Corps, 2:32–3:36, http://www.youtube.com/watch?v=N6PljcpfL38.

"WAAC's Officer's Cap." A history of the hat worn in the Women's Army Auxiliary Corps, unofficially known as the "Hobby Hat," http://americanhistory.si.edu/militaryhistory/collection/object.asp?ID=805&utm_source=twitter&utm_medium=twitter&utm_campaign=thisdayinhistory.

"WAC Head Sworn In." 1942. Budget Films Stock Footage. Video footage of Oveta Culp Hobby's swearing-in ceremony for the Women's Army Corps and a short speech she gives afterward, http://www.budgetfilms.com/clip/8122/.

Woman's Christian Temperance Union, http://wctu.org/.

Women's Army Auxiliary Corps (3:13) TV-14. The History Channel. Documentary footage promotional video celebrating the first anniversary of the founding of the WAACs, May 14, 1943, http://www.history.com/videos/womens-army-auxiliary-corps#womens-army-auxiliary-corps.

Women's Army Corps. A brief video comparing women in the Army today with the original Women's Army Corps. Contains a retrospective from several members of the original Women's Army Corps, http://www.youtube.com/watch?v=z_Y8zxsOsks&feature=related.

The Women's Army Corps, 1945–1978, by Bettie J. Morden, Center for

Military History, U.S. Army, http://www.history.army.mil
/books/wac/index.htm.

The Women's Army Corps: A Commemoration of World War II Service. Judith A. Bellafaire. CMH Publication 72-15. U.S. Army Center of Military History, http://www.history.army.mil/brochures/WAC/WAC.HTM.

Women at War, Part 1: Women's Army Corps. Promotional recruitment video made in conjunction with the U.S. Army, http://www.youtube.com/watch?v=ALow_k85n2s.

Women at War, Part 2: Women's Army Corps. Promotional recruitment video made in conjunction with the U.S. Army, http://www.youtube.com/watch?v=efCMW1qOiks&feature=related.

Women at War, Part 3: Women's Army Corps. Colonel Oveta Culp Hobby gives the graduation address to the officer's class of the Women's Army Corps (her speech starts at 1:36), http://www.youtube.com/watch?v=XxML6I2JGbo.

Selected Bibliography

★

Assistant to President Dwight D. Eisenhower to Oveta Culp Hobby, letter dated August 5, 1955. Woodson Research Center, Fondren Library, Rice University, Houston, Texas.

Associated Press Biographical Service. "Mrs. Oveta Culp Hobby." Sketch 3820, July 15, 1953, New York.

Bandel, Betty. Letter of August 27, 1995. Woodson Research Center, Fondren Library, Rice University, Houston, Texas.

———. "Letter of Betty Bandel prepared in November, 1942, to inform her family of her trip to England with Mrs. Eleanor Roosevelt and Colonel Oveta Culp Hobby," November 19, 1942. Oveta Culp Hobby Memorial Library Archives, Killeen, Texas.

Barnes, Marguerite Johnston. "Eulogy for Oveta Culp Hobby," 1995. Houston, Texas. Woodson Research Center, Fondren Library, Rice University, Houston, Texas.

———. "KPRC note," 1986. Woodson Research Center, Fondren Library, Rice University, Houston, Texas.

———. "Oveta Culp Hobby Biography, First Draft," undated. Woodson Research Center, Fondren Library, Rice University, Houston, Texas.

Barron, James. "Oveta Culp Hobby, Founder of the WACs and First Secretary of Health, Dies at 90." *New York Times,* August 17, 1995. http://www.nytimes.com/1995/08/17/obituaries/oveta-culp-hobby -founder-of-the-wacs-and-first-secretary-of-health-dies-at-90 .html.

Beckworth, Laura. Oral interview, Hobby Foundation offices, November 19, 2009. Houston, Texas.

Bentsen, Lloyd. Letter of August 29, 1995. Woodson Research Center, Fondren Library, Rice University, Houston, Texas.

"Birthday Fellows." *Time*, November 30, 1953.

"A Boost for Poor Brother." *Time*, February 3, 1967.

"Bootleg Report." *Time*, February 25, 1957.

Braden, Joan. *Just Enough Rope: An Intimate Memoir*. New York: Villard Books, 1989.

Bugbee, Sylvia J., ed. *An Officer and a Lady: The World War II Letters of Lt. Col. Betty Bandel, Women's Army Corps*. Hanover, New Hampshire: University Press of New England, 2004.

Carleton, Don. E. *Red Scare: Right-Wing Hysteria, Fifties Fanaticism and Their Legacy in Texas*. Austin, Texas: Texas Monthly Press, 1985.

Carrington, Evelyn M., ed. *Women in Early Texas*. Denton, Texas: Texas State Historical Association, 1994.

Clark, James Anthony, and Weldon Hart. *The Tactful Texan: A Biography of Governor Will Hobby*. New York: Random House, 1958.

Cole, Martha. "First WAC Head Now Busy Publisher." *St. Louis Post-Dispatch*, August 28, 1947.

Collier, Everett. "Hobby Husband-Wife Team Rates High Here." *Houston Chronicle*, October 12, 1951.

Cox, Patrick. *The First Texas News Barons*. Austin: University of Texas Press, 2005.

Crawford, Ann Fears, and Crystal Sasse Ragsdale. *Women in Texas*. Austin, Texas: State House Press, 1992.

"Crusade Staff Summoned to Friday Parley: Workers Called to Map Campaign Plans by Oveta Culp Hobby." *Houston Post*, October 5, 1934, 1.

"Department of Health and Human Services Timeline of Growth." Cato Institute, Washington, DC. http://www.downsizingthegovernment.org/hhs/timeline.

Duncan, Gra'Delle. "Killeen: Tale of Two Cities 1882–1982." *Killeen Daily Herald*, 1984, Killeen, Texas.

Duncan, Patsy. "Young Oveta was 'Decidedly Different.'" *Killeen Daily Herald*, 1986, Killeen, Texas.

Dunlap, Katherine. "Oveta Hobby, Boss of HEW." *The Philadelphia Inquirer Magazine*, November 8, 1953, 9–12.

Fernea, Elizabeth W., and Marilyn P. Duncan, eds. *Texas Women in Politics*. Austin, Texas: Foundation for Women's Resources, Inc, 1977.

"First Anniversary of Women's Army Auxiliary Corps—Address Delivered by Col. Oveta Culp Hobby, Director." Speech given to the Texas State Society of Washington, D.C., recorded in Appendix to the Congressional Record, U.S. House of Representatives, May 17, 1943, A2461-A2465.

Goldwater, Senator Barry, to Oveta Culp Hobby, letter marked "Personal," June 6, 1955. Woodson Research Center, Fondren Library, Rice University, Houston, Texas.

Gregory, Chester W. *Women in Defense Work During World War II: An Analysis of the Labor Problem and Women's Rights*. Jericho, New York: Exposition Press, 1974.

Hardy, Ann. "Oveta Culp to Carry Family Banner in Race." *Houston Post-Dispatch*, June 24, 1930.

"The Heir Apparent." *Time*, May 30, 1960. (Re: Bill Hobby Jr. named managing editor of the *Houston Post*.)

Hobby, Bill, and Saralee Tiede. *How Things Really Work: Lessons from a Life in Politics*. Austin, Texas: Dolph Briscoe Center for American History, University of Texas at Austin, 2010.

Hobby, Diana. Oral interview, Hobby Foundation offices, November 19, 2009, Houston, Texas.

"Hobby Out." *Time*, July 23, 1945.

Hobby, Oveta Culp. "Around the World in 13 Days with Oveta Culp Hobby." *Houston Post*, 1947.

———. Letter to Helen Johnson, dated August 11, 1943 and October 7, 1943. Woodson Research Center, Fondren Library, Rice University, Houston, Texas.

———. Letter to Senator Thomas Desmond, dated January 25, 1961. Woodson Research Center, Fondren Library, Rice University, Houston, Texas.

———. *Mr. Chairman: Rules, and Examples in Story Form, of Parliamentary Procedure Written Expressly for Use in Schools and Clubs*. Fort Worth, Texas: The Economy Company, 1936.

———. Speech at formal opening of the Aquinas Student Center, Sacred Heart Dominical College, April 10, 1960. Woodson

Research Center, Fondren Library, Rice University, Houston, Texas.

———. Telegram to William P. Hobby Jr., August 18, 1995. Woodson Research Center, Fondren Library, Rice University, Houston, Texas.

"Hobby Sends Word to Namesake: WACs Hurdled Many Road-blocks." *Texas Woman's University*, newsletter, volume 1, number 2, Summer 1983.

"Hobby, William Pettus." *Handbook of Texas Online*, http://www .tshaonline.org/handbook/online/articles/fho04.

Hobby, William P., Jr. "Oveta Culp Hobby." *Handbook of Texas Online*, 1996, http://www.tshaonline.org/handbook/online /articles/fho86.

"Hobby's Army." *Time*, January 17, 1944.

Hunter, Helen, Denise Nosal, and Mary Gillette, eds. "Oveta Culp Hobby." In *Houston Women from Suffrage to City Hall*, 18–21. Houston, Texas: League of Voters of Houston Education Fund, 1987.

Hurt, Harry III. "The Last of the Great Ladies." *Texas Monthly*, October 1978, 142–148, 225–238.

Hutchison, Kay Bailey. *American Heroines: The Spirited Women Who Shaped Our Country*. New York: HarperCollins, 2004.

"Jesse Jones, 3 Others Saved As Pilots Land Burning Plane." *Washington Post*, June 13, 1936.

Johnson, Bobby H. "Oral History Interview with Clarice Fortgang Pollard." April 18, 1985. Stephen F. Austin State University Oral History Program, World War II Project. Nacogdoches, Texas.

Johnson, Helen. Letters to Oveta Culp Hobby, dated March 6, 1942; March 17, 1943; March 22, 1943; March 31, 1943; and August 9, 1943. Woodson Research Center, Fondren Library, Rice University, Houston, Texas.

Johnson, Lyndon B. "Message to Mrs. Oveta Culp Hobby on the Death of Former Governor William P. Hobby of Texas." The American Presidency Project, 1964, http://www.presidency.ucsb .edu/ws/index.php?pid=26301.

Johnston, Marguerite. *Houston: The Unknown City, 1836–1946*. College Station, Texas: Texas A&M University Press, 1991.

———. Phone interview with Oveta Culp Hobby, June 26, 1985. Woodson Research Center, Fondren Library, Rice University, Houston, Texas.

———. Undated interview with Oveta Culp Hobby. Woodson Research Center, Fondren Library, Rice University, Houston, Texas.

Kirkland, Kate Sayen. *The Hogg Family and Houston: Philanthropy and the Civic Ideal.* Austin: University of Texas Press, 2009.

Kochebdoerfer, Violet A. *One Woman's World War II.* Lexington: The University Press of Kentucky, 1994.

Koidin, Michelle. "Friends, Dignitaries Laud Oveta Culp Hobby," *Austin American-Statesman,* August 19, 1995.

———. "Oveta Culp Hobby Dies after Life of Service: 'Little Colonel' Blazed Trail from Texas Capitol to Pentagon, White House." *Austin American-Statesman,* August 17, 1995.

"Lady in Command." *Time,* May 4, 1953.

Lasher, Patricia, and Beverly Bentley. *Texas Women—Interviews and Images.* Austin, Texas: Shoal Creek Publishers, 1980.

LeFew-Blake, Penelope A. *Fort Des Moines.* Charleston, South Carolina: Arcadia Publishing, 2006.

Limmer, E. A. Jr., ed. *Story of Bell County, Texas, Volume II.* Austin, Texas: Eakin Press, 1988.

Marler, Charles H. "William Hobby and Oveta Hobby." In *American Newspaper Publishers 1950–1990,* ed. Perry J. Ashley. Detroit, Michigan: Gale Research, 1993.

McComb, David G. Personal interview with Oveta Culp Hobby, July 11, 1969. Hobby family papers, private collection. Houston, Texas.

"Milestones." *Time,* August 28, 1995 (obituary).

Mills, C. Wright. *The Power Elite: New Edition.* New York: Oxford University Press, 2000.

Morden, Bettie J. *The Women's Army Corps: 1945–1978.* Washington, D.C.: United States Army Center of Military History, 1990.

"Mrs. Hobby Now Wields Quieter Form of Clout." *Victoria Advocate,* May 15, 1988.

"Mrs. Hobby Sends Thanks to Killeen." *Killeen Daily Herald,* January 19, 1986.

"Mrs. Secretary Hobby." *Time,* May 4, 1953. Volume LXI, number 18.

Murray, Alexander S. *Who's Who in Mythology: A Classic Guide to the Ancient World*. New York: Bonanza Books, 1988.

Myers, Dee Dee. *Why Women Should Rule the World*. New York: Harper, 2008.

Norman, Mrs. T. H. "Lady of Killeen." Unpublished article, October 1954. Woodson Research Center, Fondren Library, Rice University, Houston, Texas.

Oldstone, Michael A. *Viruses, Plagues, and History*. New York: Oxford University Press, 2000.

"Oveta Culp Hobby." *Texas Alcalde*, November/December 1995, 59 (obituary).

"Oveta Culp Hobby." U.S. Army Women's Museum, Fort Lee, Virginia, http://www.awm.lee.army.mil/research-pages/hobby.htm.

Oveta Culp Hobby papers. Woodson Research Center, Fondren Library, Rice University, Houston, Texas.

"Oveta Culp Hobby to Publish Simplified Parliamentary Law." *Dallas Times-Herald*, October 11, 1936.

"Oveta Culp Hobby's New Job." *Business Week*, May 16, 1953, 116–121.

Pando, Robert. "Oveta Culp Hobby." Doctoral dissertation, Florida State University, Tallahassee. 2008.

Roosevelt, Eleanor. *This I Remember*. New York: Greenwood Press Reprint, 1975.

Rosenblatt, Robert. "Letting Bad Enough Alone." *Time*, October 13, 1980. (Article on public gaffes. "And there was OCH, who, as Secretary of Health, Education and Welfare in 1955, explained the shortage of the new Salk vaccine: 'No one could have foreseen its great acclaim.'")

Sallee, Rad. "Hobby Remembered as a Dignified Leader, Innovative Publisher." *Houston Chronicle*, August 17, 1995.

"Selective Service System." http://www.sss.gov/backgr.htm.

Serrin, Judith. "Advice to Cabinet Women." *Detroit Free Press*, January 19, 1977.

Shannon, Michael. "They Built Houston." *Houston Town and Country*, April 1976.

Shire, Al, ed. *Oveta Culp Hobby*. Houston, Texas: Western Lithograph, 1997.

"Short Takes." *Time*, June 19, 1972. (Re: The *Houston Post* endorsing Bill Hobby Jr. in runoff for lieutenant governor nomination.)

Sills, Rebekah. "'We Shall Not Fail Freedom:' Oveta Culp Hobby's Role in the Implementation and Formation of the Women's Army Corps During World War II." Master's Thesis, Baylor University, Waco, Texas, 2007.

"Stepsister Corps." *Time*, May 10, 1943.

"Stimson Condemns Gossip About WAAC; Secretary Asserts Immorality Charges Are 'Absolutely and Completely False.'" *New York Times*, June 11, 1943, 6.

Sutphen, Debra Lynn. "Conservative Warrior: Oveta Culp Hobby and the Administration of America's Health, Education, and Welfare, 1953–1955." Dissertation, Washington State University, Pullman, Washington, 1997.

Thomas, Lanny. "Man in a Flying Machine." *Shreveport Times*, March 3, 1968.

"Three for the Post." *Time*, March 1, 1963. (Re: *Houston Post* buying *Galveston News*, *Galveston Tribune*, and *Texas City Sun*.)

Todd, Lewis Paul, and Merle Eugene Curti. *Rise of The American Nation*, 3rd edition. New York: Harcourt Brace Jovanovich, 1972.

Treadwell, Mattie E. *United States Army in World War II Special Studies: The Women's Army Corps*. CMH Pub. 11–8, Office of the Chief of Military History, Department of the Army, Washington, D.C.

Tyler, Ron, Janice Pinney, and Colleen Kain. *Proceedings of the Annual Meeting at Corpus Christi: December 1–3, 1995*. Austin, Texas: The Philosophical Society of Texas, 1996.

"WAAC: U.S. Women Troops to Enlist in Army's First All-Female Force." *Life*, June 8, 1942.

"WAC's Colonel Hobby." *Time*, January 17, 1944. Volume XLIII, number 3.

Wakefield, Eleanor. "Mrs. Hobby, Back Home, Asserts Freedom Means 'Right to Know.'" *Houston Chronicle*, May 23, 1948.

"Where She Is and Where She's Going." *Time*, March 20, 1972.

"Who Will Get the Vaccine." *Time*, April 25, 1955.

Woodbury, Clarence. "America's Glamorous Godmother." *The American Magazine*, May 1953.

Index

Page numbers in italics indicate photos.

Alabama Press Association, 55

American Export Lines, 40

American Farm Federation Convention, 29

American Medical Association, 94

American Society of Newspaper Editors, 22

Army-Navy Club, 36

Army Quartermaster Corps, 35

Associated Press, 87

Austin, Texas, 12, 13, 17

Bandel, Betty, 37–38, 40–41, 43, 45–46, 49

Baraban, Joe, 78

Beckworth, Laura Hobby, *80*, 89–90

Ben Wold's Fashion, 28

Berlin, Irving, 48

Bethune, Mary McLeod, *37*

Bowman, Pat, 88, 91

Braden, Joan, 67–69, 84

Brown, George, 88

Brown v. Board of Education, 79

Burgoyne, Wally, 46

Business Week, 58

Butler, George, 25

Caesarean section, 19, 22

Capitol Hill, 31, 36

Catto, Henry, *80*, 81

Catto, Jessica Hobby, *16*, 22, 45, *80*, 81, 91

Chaplin, Charlie, 55

Chautauqua, 8

Chicago, 29

Citizens for Eisenhower, 56

Claridge's, 41

Cockrill, Kimberly, x

Communism, 54, 55

Congressional Record, 5

Connally, Tom, 14

Crowther, Jim, 90

Culp, Emma Elizabeth Hoover, 2–4, 6, 9, 17

Culp, Ike W., 2–3, 6–9, 12, 17, 18

Culp, John Robinson, 3

Culp, Juanita, 4

Culp, Rachel Eaton, 3

Cutter Biologicals, 64–65

Dallas, 14, 20

Degas, 88

Democratic Club, 13

Democrats, 55, 57

Democrats for Eisenhower, 56

139

Department of Health, Education, and Welfare (HEW), ix, 58–59, *60*, 61, 65–67, *69*, 74, 79, 84, 88, 93
Distinguished Service Medal, 48, *52*
Doctor's Hospital, 49
Dolph Briscoe Center for American History, 78, 80
Dr. Turner's Neurological Center, 24

Economy Company, 22
Eisenhower, Dwight D., 43–44, 48, 56–58, *60*, 62, *63*, 68, *69*, 72–75, 77, 94
Eisenhower Republican, 55
Elkins, James A., 23–24, 26

Federal Communications Commission, 23, 24, 26
Federal Security Administration, 57
Ferguson, Jim, 5–6
Folsom, Marion B., 73
Food and Drug Administration, 58
Fort Des Moines, Iowa, 36–37, 44
Fort Hood, 84
Fort Sam Houston, 44
Fortune, 88
Foynes, Ireland, 40
Fuermann, George, 55

Giza, Cairo, Egypt, 46, *47*
Goldwater, Barry, 65
Great Depression, 14, 47
Gris, 88
Guy, Jeanne, x

H&C Communications, 85–86
Hefley, Edwin, 20–21
Hitler, Adolph, 30
Hobby, Bill (William, Jr.), *16*, 19, 45, 58, *80*, 81, 91, 93
Hobby, Diana, *80*, 81
Hobby, Oveta Culp, ix, 2, *16*, 17, 19, 20–25, 27, 83–84, 86–87, *92*, 93, 95–96; Colonel, xiv, 1, 2, 33, *37*, 38, *42*, 43–46, *47*, 48–51, *52*, 89, 90–91; Culp, Oveta, 2–9, *10*, 11–13, 17–18; Director, WAAC, 33–37, 39–40, 44, 93; Executive vice president, *Houston Post*, 53–56; Federal Security Administration, 57; Parliamentarian, *10*, 11–12, 15, 18; Philanthropist, 88–89; Publisher, *Houston Post*, 78, 79–80, *80*, 81–82, *82*, 85–86; Secretary, Department of Health, Education and Welfare, 58–59, *60*, 61, 62, *63*, 63–68, *63*, *69*, *69*, *70*, *71*, 72, *72*, 73–77, 79, 87–88, 94; Women's Army Auxiliary Corps, 30–33; Women's Interest Section, 27–30
Hobby, Paul, *80*
Hobby, William P., 2, 5–6, *7*, 9, *16*, 17–21, 23–25, 27–30, 32, 49, 55–56, 58–59, *60*, 67–68, 72–73, 79–81, 88, 90–91
Hobby Foundation, 89
"Hobby Hat," 35
House Resolution 4906, 30
Houston, Texas, 12–13, 15, 53, 66, 73, 79, 91
Houston Chronicle, 23
Houston Club, 28

Houston Post, 12, 19, 21–22, 26, 53, 55–56, 59, 67, 78, 79–80, 84–85, 88
Houston Post-Dispatch, 17, 19
Houston Red Scare, 59
Houston Symphony Orchestra Committee, 19, 53
Hughes, Sarah T., 14
Humphrey, George M., 72
Hutchison, Kay Bailey, 80–81
Huyser, Cindy, x

Johnson, Lady Bird, 24, 81, 90
Johnson, Lyndon Baines, 19, 24, 57, 81–82, *82*, 90
Johnston, Marguerite, 55, 66–67
Jones, Jesse, 22
Jones, Nancy Baker, x
Junior League, 19

Kennedy, John F., 96
Killeen, Texas, 1–3, 6, 82–84
Kilman, Ed, 55–56, 59
KLEE, 23–24
KPRC, 26, 80–81, 85

League of Women Voters, 18, 79
Lee, W. Albert, 23–24, 26
"Little Colonel," 43–45
Long, Mary Day, x
Lord & Taylor, 87
Loving, Lynn Culp, 1–3, 8, 28

Marini, Marino, 89
Marshall, George C., 29–32, 36, 51
Mary Hardin-Baylor College, 8, 12
Matisse, Henri, 88
Matisse, Pierre, 53, 88
May, Theresa, ix
McAllister, Marty, x
McCarthy, Joe, 55

Mills, C. Wright, 93
Minute Women, 55, 59
Miró, Joan, 88
Mobilization for Human Needs, 19
Modigliani, 88
Moody, Dan, 12
Mr. Chairman, 21–22
Museum of Fine Arts Houston, 19, 53, 88

National Democratic Convention, 13
National Health Reinsurance Program, 94
National Institutes of Health, 64
Nazism, 54
New York City, 56
New York World's Fair, 22
Nineteenth Amendment, 9

Office of Education, 58
Office of Vocational Rehabilitation, 58
O'Leary, Ralph, 59
Oveta Culp Hobby Memorial Library, ix, 68, 82

Pando, Robert, x
Parliamentary procedure, 11–12
Pearl Harbor, 29–30
Perkins, Frances, 87
Picasso, Pablo, 89
Pierce, P. J., x
Polio, 61, 64–68
Public Health Service, 58

"Reds," 54–55
Republicans, 57
Roberson, Pat, 84
Rogers, Edith Nourse, 30–31

Roosevelt, Eleanor, 40, 44
Roosevelt, Franklin D., 20, 30, 32, 47, 87

Sabin, Albert, 62–64
Salk, Jonas, 62–63, 63, 64, 66–67, 70, 71, 73–74
Sanders, Marc, x
Schacher, Eugene, 20–21
Scheele, Leonard, 64, 67–68
Senate Finance Committee, 58
Smith, Kate, 42, 48
Snyder, Murry, 74
Social Security Act, 57
Social Security Administration, 58
Stimson, Henry, 30–31, 36, 48, 52
St. Louis Dispatch, 54
Stone, Ron, 85–86
Surles, Alexander Day, 26–28

Temperance, 4
Temple, Texas, 6, 8, 14, 18
Temple High School, 8
Texas Banking Commission, 14
Texas Business Hall of Fame, 85
Texas House of Representatives, 12
Texas legislature, 7, 10–11, 13
Texas Medical Center, 67
Texas Monthly, 84
Time magazine, 58
Toronto Sun Publishing Company, 84
Treadwell, Mattie E., 90

Unitarian, 15
University of Texas, 12–13, 80

Walee Laundry, 24
War bonds, 42, 47–48
War Department, 40, 45
War Department Bureau of Public Relations, 26, 29–31
Washington, D.C., 26, 28, 30, 33, 59, 88
Washington Post, 86
Weather Channel, 86
White House Conference on Education, 74
Winegarten, Alvin, x
Winegarten, Debra L., 83
Winegarten, Ruthe, ii, v, x
Women's Army Corps, ix, 39, 44–46, 48–50, 75, 79, 82, 90, 93, 95
Women's Auxiliary Army Corps, 1, 29–37, 39, 41, 43–44, 95
Women's Christian Temperance Union, 3
Women's Crusade, 22
Women's Interest Section, 26, 29
Woodson Research Center, Fondren Library, Rice University, 70, 71
Woodson Research Center Special Collections Archives, ix
World War II, 1, 26, 30, 42, 48, 50, 54, 56, 88

Young, Jim, 14–15

CPSIA information can be obtained
at www.ICGtesting.com
Printed in the USA
FSOW01n0212110216
16752FS